RADIUS

RADIUS

Jonathan Hassell

O'REILLY®

Beijing · Cambridge · Farnham · Köln · Paris · Sebastopol · Taipei · Tokyo

RADIUS
by Jonathan Hassell

Published by O'Reilly Media, Inc., 1005 Gravenstein Highway North, Sebastopol, CA 95472.

O'Reilly Media, Inc. books may be purchased for educational, business, or sales promotional use. On-line editions are also available for most titles (*safari.oreilly.com*). For more information, contact our corporate/institutional sales department: (800) 998-9938 or *corporate@oreilly.com*.

Editor:	Jim Sumser
Production Editor:	Darren Kelly
Cover Designer:	Hanna Dyer
Interior Designer:	David Futato
Production Services:	Octal Publishing, Inc.

Printing History:

October 2002:	First Edition.

 This book uses RepKover,™ a durable and flexible lay-flat binding.

ISBN: 0-596-00322-6

Table of Contents

Preface

"Trust no one."

Aside from being the motto and *modus operandi* for the successful TV series *The X Files*, it is also a beneficial mantra to practice in all facets of security and investigation. Even though chances are good that you won't encounter Mulder, Scully, and their gang, they still teach a concept that's become increasingly relevant as the world—and the world's computers—become connected.

Companies today are increasingly basing their business models around providing access to resources—web pages, Internet access, email accounts, or anything else—that need to be protected. How does a user indicate to a system, especially one that indeed trusts no one, that he's entitled to use that computer's services? How can the owner of a business keep non-paying users out of the way while providing convenient access to paying customers? The bottom line is this: with new security exploits being uncovered every day and the general environment of the Internet public degenerating from a trusted environment into one of hostility and attack, there has to be some way in which an Internet citizen can use resources to which he's entitled without letting everybody else in the gates.

This is the purpose of the RADIUS protocol—to differentiate, secure, and account for these users. And the purpose of this book is to provide the most complete reference to RADIUS possible.

Audience

This book is designed to serve all manner of readers. There's enough introductory information to give a complete, generalized background for the administrator not familiar with the protocol. There's practical, day-to-day, hands-on information for those tasked with configuring and using RADIUS servers. There's design-level information for programmers who need to write custom applications to integrate RADIUS. In other words, there's something in this book for everyone.

Organization

I have tried to structure this book as effectively as possible, mixing theory with practice where appropriate, so you, the reader, have a firm background with which to apply both the practical advice and procedures in this book and others you may develop on your own.

Chapter 1, *An Overview of RADIUS*, takes a few steps backward and looks at the architectural model on which the RADIUS protocol is based, provides an introduction to RADIUS's characteristics and limitations, and offers a brief discussion of its history.

Chapter 2, *RADIUS Specifics*, details the individual characteristics of the RADIUS protocol, including an overview of its standard packet formats and the structure of the properties it passes to various servers, as well as a discussion of how vendors extend the functionality of the protocol through the use of their own defined attributes. There is also commentary on the various authentication protocols that can be used in conjunction with RADIUS, as well as a brief introduction to the hints file.

Chapter 3, *Standard RADIUS Attributes*, is a reference section for all of the globally defined RADIUS attributes as specified in the appropriate RFC documents. An "at a glance" chart details each attribute's primary properties with a short discussion of its purpose. Any special behaviors that an administrator might encounter during its use are covered in this discussion.

Chapter 4, *RADIUS Accounting*, is presented as a combination of the stylistic elements of Chapters 2 and 3 and covers the properties, behaviors, and attributes of the accounting portion of the RADIUS protocol. It discusses standard accounting packets, proxy functionality, and the standard accounting attributes as specified by the RFCs.

Chapter 5, *Getting Started with FreeRADIUS*, is the first hands-on chapter in the book. It discusses obtaining, installing, configuring, and using FreeRADIUS, an open source RADIUS server that was created in part by several developers of the Debian Linux distribution.

Chapter 6, *Advanced FreeRADIUS*, continues the practical guidance and covers the more intimate and intricate configuration options that FreeRADIUS provides. In addition, extending FreeRADIUS's functionality is covered, by having it authenticate against a MySQL database, use the pluggable authentication module (PAM) in its transactions, and interact with Cisco networking gear. Simultaneous use, also known as multilinking in the ISP business, is also covered.

Chapter 7, *Other RADIUS Applications*, discusses other programs to augment FreeRADIUS, including an Apache module that will allow the web server to authenticate against the RADIUS user database, a powerful email and directory server that will consolidate user information and reduce administrative headaches, and a utility for parsing and analyzing RADIUS log files.

Chapter 8, *The Security of RADIUS*, is a commentary on some of the security problems the protocol has and how to work around them. Unfortunately, the protocol used to secure networks has some vulnerabilities of its own, and this chapter offers insight into what the vulnerabilities are, how they were introduced, and what an administrator can do to eliminate the potential threat they represent.

Chapter 9, *New RADIUS Developments*, includes information that's not present in the original RFC documents for the protocol. Among these new details are information on tunnel support, Apple networking support, interim accounting updates, using Extensible Authentication Protocol (EAP), and a listing—like that of Chapter 3—of the new attributes added by the RADIUS Extensions RFC.

Chapter 10, *Deployment Techniques*, concludes the book by offering design guidelines and practical suggestions for planning a RADIUS server deployment in your organization. Topics include services, availability, system baselining, and proactive/reactive system management.

The Appendix is a list of all of the RADIUS attributes covered within the book, a few of their key properties, and cross-references by page number.

Conventions Used in This Book

- *Italic* is used for filenames, directories, URLs, emphasis, and the first use of technical terms.
- `Constant width` is used for IP addresses, configuration file operators, and packet names and attributes.
- **`Constant width bold`** is used for user input.

 This icon designates a note, which is an important aside to nearby text.

 This icon designates a warning relating to the nearby text.

How to Contact Us

Please address comments and questions concerning this book to the publisher:

O'Reilly & Associates, Inc.
1005 Gravenstein Highway North
Sebastopol, CA 95472
(800) 998-9938 (in the United States or Canada)
(707) 829-0515 (international or local)
(707) 829-0104 (fax)

We have a web page for this book, where we list errata, examples, or any additional information. You can access this page at:

http://www.oreilly.com/catalog/RADIUS

To comment or ask technical questions about this book, send email to:

bookquestions@oreilly.com

For more information about our books, conferences, Resource Centers, and the O'Reilly Network, see our web site at:

http://www.oreilly.com

The author has created a comprehensive web site to support this book, located at *http://www.theradiusbook.com*. You can find an overview, the table of contents, a listing of errata, sample code, and many other resources at that site.

Acknowledgments

A variety of people came together to make this book possible. My publisher, O'Reilly, has made the writing and production of this book proceed as smoothly as possible. I'd also like to extend heartfelt thanks to my editor, Jim Sumser. I've sat here for an hour attempting to come up with fifty words that could adequately describe what a genuinely fine man Mr. Sumser is, and I conclude it's not possible. Rarely in life are you provided an opportunity to work with such a gentleman and professional. Jim defines those qualities, and I am better for it.

I'd also like to thank the fine folks at Equipment Data Associates (EDA) in Charlotte, North Carolina for offering me an opportunity to work and write. The flexibility I was granted in working with EDA was a godsend and delayed the onset of gray hair on me by at least two years. Mason Dunlap, my supervisor, and Bill Howell, a long-time friend, neighbor, and role model, were particularly encouraging and even interested (or at least they did a fabulous job of feigning said interest) in the progress of the book. My debt of gratitude to them is enormous.

Mike and Debbie Hassell, my father and mother, were also supportive and caring. I hope I do justice to their expectations. Thanks also to Aaron and Julie Slyter for their friendship, Tom Syroid for the inspiration to write books, and Robert Bruce Thompson for guidance.

Special thanks to Alan DeKok of the FreeRADIUS project and Niels Jonker of Boingo Wireless for their timely and Herculean efforts to review this book. I believe I owe both of them a couple of beers.

Last but by no means least, my longtime girlfriend, Anna Watson, was by my side through thick and thin and suffered through more than one weekend during which I was focused on email and chapter writing instead of romantic dinners and movie watching. I suspect she will require an approval form signed in triplicate before I write another book. (Who can blame her?) This book would never have gotten off the ground were it not for her support and love.

## CHAPTER 1

An Overview of RADIUS

In an ideal world, we wouldn't have to use authentication of any type to gain access to anything. But as long as free enterprise exists and access to private resources is sold, authentication will exist.

You may have experienced authentication as recently as an hour ago, when you used a dial-up Internet account to log on and surf the Web for the latest headlines. You may have checked your corporate email on your PalmPilot to see if your biggest client had returned your message about the newest proposal. And this weekend, when you use a VPN to connect to your office network so you can revise that presentation that's due early Monday morning, you'll have to authenticate yourself.

But what goes on behind the scenes when you prove your identity to a computer? After all, the computer has to have a set of processes and protocols to verify that you are indeed who you say you are, find out what you are allowed to access, and finally, tell you all of this. There's one protocol that does this all: the Remote Access Dialin User Service, or RADIUS.

RADIUS, originally developed by Livingston Enterprises, is an access-control protocol that verifies and authenticates users based on the commonly used challenge/response method. (I'll talk more about challenge/response authentication later.) While RADIUS has a prominent place among Internet service providers, it also belongs in any environment where central authentication, regulated authorization, and detailed user accounting is needed or desired.

An Overview of AAA

The framework around which RADIUS is built is known as the AAA process, consisting of authentication, authorization, and accounting. While there's nothing specific to RADIUS in the AAA model, a general background is needed to justify most of RADIUS's behavior. RADIUS was created before the AAA model was developed, but it was the first real AAA-based protocol exhibiting the AAA functionality to earn industry acceptance and widespread use. However, that's not to say there aren't other protocols that satisfy the architecture's requirements.

This model serves to manage and report all transactions from start to finish. The following questions serve well as a mimicking of the functionality by asking:

- Who are you?
- What services am I allowed to give you?
- What did you do with my services while you were using them?

To begin, let's look at why the AAA architecture is a better overall strategy than others. Before AAA was introduced, individual equipment had to be used to authenticate users. Without a formal standard, each machine likely had a different method of authentication—some might have used profiles, while others might have used Challenge/Handshake Authentication Protocol (CHAP) authentication, and still others might have queried a small internal database with SQL. The major problem with this helter-skelter model is one of scalability: while keeping track of users on one piece of network equipment might not be a huge manageability obstacle, increasing capacity by adding other equipment (each with its own authentication methods) quickly ballooned the process into a nightmare. Kludgy scripts were written to halfway automate the process, but there was no real way to monitor usage, automatically authenticate users, and seamlessly provide a variety of services.

The AAA Working Group was formed by the IETF to create a functional architecture that would address the limitations of the system described above. Obviously, there was a need to focus on decentralizing equipment and monitoring usage in heterogeneous networks. ISPs began offering services other than just standard dial-up, including ISDN, xDSL, and cable-modem connectivity, and there needed to be a standard way in which users could be verified, logged on, and monitored throughout the network. After much work, the AAA architecture was born.

The AAA model focuses on the three crucial aspects of user access control: authentication, authorization, and accounting, respectively. I will now take a closer look at each of these steps.

Authentication

Authentication is the process of verifying a person's (or machine's) declared identity. You're familiar with the most common form of authentication, using a combination of logon ID and a password, in which the knowledge of the password is a representation that the user is authentic. Distributing the password, however, destroys this method of authenticating, which prompted creators of e-commerce sites and other Internet-business transactors to require a stronger, more reliable authenticator. Digital certificates are one of the solutions here, and over the next five to ten years it's likely that using digital certificates as a part of the public key infrastructure (PKI) will become the preferred authenticator on the Internet.

A Word About Terminology

When discussing AAA and RADIUS, the terms "client" and "server" often come up. However, there can be some confusion about which of these roles a particular machine is playing in a specific transaction. Let's take a look at each of these roles.

A *client*, in the traditional sense, is a machine that makes requests of and uses resources on another machine. In the AAA framework, and with RADIUS specifically, the client can be the end user who wants to connect to a network's resources—in other words, a service consumer. However, in another context, an AAA client can be the machine that sends AAA-style packets to and from an AAA server. This is the strictest sense of the "client" term.

A *server* is commonly known as the machine of which clients request resources. In AAA, this can be the network server—a NAS machine or some other concentrator— or an AAA server that authenticates, authorizes, and performs accounting functions. How the word "server" is meant really depends on the context of the architecture on which the discussion is based.

In this book, I will use the contextually based meanings of these terms interchangeably, as there is no clear-cut and non-kludgy method to provide any additional degree of consistency. I have tried to specifically identify clients and servers as AAA or RADIUS clients and servers where possible.

The key aspect of authentication is that it allows two unique objects to form a *trust relationship*—both are assumed to be valid users. Trust between systems allows for such key functionality as proxy servers, in which a system grants a request on behalf of another system and allows AAA implementations to span heterogeneous networks supporting different types of clients and services. Trust relationships can become quite complex, and I'll talk more about them in a later section.

Authorization

Authorization involves using a set of rules or other templates to decide what an authenticated user can do on a system. For example, in the case of an Internet service provider, it may decide whether a static IP address is given as opposed to a DHCP-assigned address. The system administrator defines these rules.

So-called "smart implementations" of AAA servers have logic that will analyze a request and grant whatever access it can, whether or not the entire request is valid. For instance, a dial-up client connects and requests multilink bonding. A generic AAA server will simply deny the entire request, but a smarter implementation will look at the request, determine that the client is only allowed one dial-up connection, and grant the one channel while refusing the other.

Accounting

Rounding out the AAA framework is accounting, which measures and documents the resources a user takes advantage of during access. This can include the amount of system time or the amount of data a user has sent and/or received during a session. Accounting is carried out by the logging of session statistics and usage information and is used for authorization control, billing, trend analysis, resource utilization, and capacity-planning activities.

Accounting data has several uses. An administrator can analyze successful requests to determine capacity and predict future system load. A business owner can track time spent on certain services and bill accordingly. A security analyzer can look at denied requests, see if a pattern emerges, and possibly ward off a hacker or free-loader. The moral here is that the accounting data is of great utility to an AAA server administrator. I'll cover many uses of accounting data and strategies for getting the most out of the logs in Chapters 4 and 7.

Key Points About AAA Architecture

The AAA architecture, simply put, is an attempt to map out a design of how the AAA pieces fit together. AAA implementations can be as simple or as complex as they need to be, mainly because of the efforts of the Internet Research Task Force (IRTF) AAA Architecture Working Group to make a model as application-neutral as possible. In other words, the AAA model is designed to work in environments with varied user requirements and equally varied network design. There are some key attributes of the model that make this possible.

First, the AAA model depends on the client/server interaction, in which a client system requests the services or resources of a server system. In simple implementations, these roles generally stick—the server never acts as the client and vice versa. Client/server environments allow for a good load-balancing design, in which high availability and response time are critical. Servers can be distributed and decentralized among the network. Contrast this with the opposite network model, a peer-to-peer (P2P) network. With P2P networks, all systems display characteristics of both client and server systems, which can introduce such demons as processing delays and unavailability.

A proxying capability is a slight variation of this. An AAA server can be configured to authorize a request or pass it along to another AAA server, which will then make the appropriate provisions or pass it along again. In essence, a proxy chain is created, in which AAA servers make requests of both clients and other AAA servers. I said "slight variation" earlier because when a server proxies another server, the originator displays the characteristics of a client. Thus, a trust relationship has to be created for each client/server hop until the request reaches equipment that provisions the needed resources.

Proxying is a very useful feature of the AAA model and a boon to enterprise and distributed network implementations, in which some AAA equipment can be configured to always proxy requests to machines in other locations. An example of proxying at its best is with an ISP reseller agreement. Often a major networking company will make a significant investment in network infrastructure and place points of presence in multiple locations. Armed with this distributed network, the company then resells to smaller ISPs that wish to expand their coverage and take advantage of a better network. The reseller has to provide some form of access control over the tangible resources in each location, but the smaller ISP doesn't wish to share personal information about its users with the reseller. In this case, a proxying AAA machine is placed at each of the reseller's points of presence, and those machines then communicate with the appropriate NAS equipment at the smaller ISP.

Clients requesting services and resources from an AAA server (and in this case, clients can include AAA proxies) can communicate with each other by using either a *hop-to-hop* or an *end-to-end transaction*. The distinction is where the trust relationship lies in the transaction chain. Consider the following circumstances to get a better picture.

In a hop-to-hop transaction, a client makes an initial request to an AAA device. At this point, there is a trust relationship between the client and the frontline AAA server. That machine determines that the request needs to be forwarded to another server in a different location, so it acts as a proxy and contacts another AAA server. Now the trust relationship is with the two AAA servers, with the frontline machine acting as the client and the second AAA machine acting as the server. It's important to note that *the trust relationship is not inherently transitive*, meaning that the initial client and the second AAA machine *do not* have a trust relationship. Figure 1-1 shows how the trusts are sequential and independent of each other.

Differing from the hop-to-hop model is the end-to-end transaction method. The key difference is, again, where the trust relationship lies—in this model, it's between the initial, requesting client and the AAA server that finally authorizes the request. In an end-to-end model, the proxy chain is still very much functional as the model doesn't necessarily mean the transaction is end-to-end: it's the trust relationship that is. Because it is poor design to pass sensitive information in proxy requests, some other mean of authenticating a request and validating data integrity is needed when the initial request jumps through the hops in the proxy chain. Most commonly, digital certificates and other PKI certifications are used in these situations. RFCs 2903 and 2905 describe the requirements of implementing end-to-end security, which is shown in Figure 1-2.

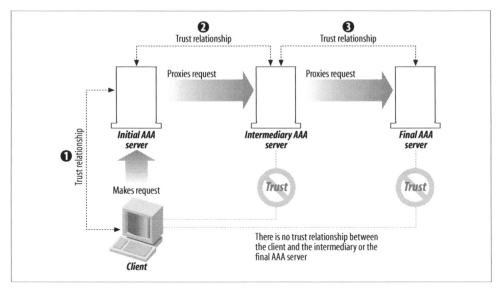

Figure 1-1. Independent trust relationships in a hop-to-hop transaction

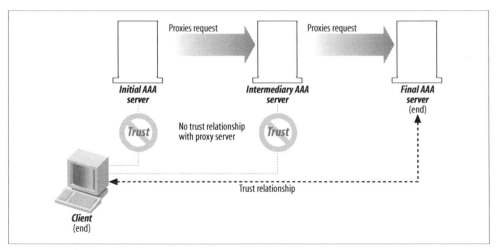

Figure 1-2. Client/server trust relationship in the end-to-end model

The Authorization Framework

Moving on in the soup of terminology, we come to the AAA Authorization Framework, an RFC document from the subset of the AAA Working Group set up by the IETF. Like an architecture document, a framework is designed as a roadmap, but it tends to be a bit more specific. Frameworks designate how systems interact with one another, but frameworks generally concentrate more on models specific to certain environments, such as an Internet wholesaler, a corporate VPN center, or other similar situations.

First, though, we should point out the distinctions in terminology. The authorization framework introduces the concept of a User Home Organization (UHO), which is an entity that has a direct contractual relationship with an end user. Also, the Service Provider (SP) is involved, which maintains and provisions the tangible network resources. The UHO and the SP need not be the same organization; a good example of this is, again, an ISP wholesaler or reseller that provides its own network resources to other organizations. For the purposes of this overview, I'll first look at scenarios in which the UHO and SP are one and the same, and then I'll cover a more detailed scenario that is commonly found.

Authorization Sequences

There are several different methods in which the end user, the AAA server, and the network equipment communicate during a transaction. Specifically, there are three different sequences in which each machine is contacted.

The agent sequence

> In this sequence, the AAA server acts as a middleman of sorts between the service equipment and the end user. The end user initially contacts the AAA server, which authorizes the user's request and sends a message to the service equipment notifying it to set that service up. The service equipment does so, notifies the AAA machine, and the notification is passed on to the end user, who then begins using the network. This sequence is typically used in broadband applications in which quality of service (QoS) is part of an existing contract.

The pull sequence

> Dial-in users frequently encounter this sequence. The end user in this situation connects directly to the service equipment (terminal gear or other NAS machinery), which then checks with an AAA server to determine whether to grant the request. The AAA server notifies the service equipment of its decision, and the service equipment then either connects or disconnects the user to the network.

The push sequence

> The push sequence alters the trust relationship between all of the machines in a transaction. The user connects to the AAA server first, and when the request to the server is authorized, the AAA server distributes some sort of authentication "receipt" (a digital certificate or signed token, perhaps) back to the end user. The end user then pushes this token along with his request to the service equipment, and the equipment treats the ticket from the AAA server as a green light to provision the service. The main distinction is that the user acts as the agent between the AAA server and the service equipment.

Here are some diagrams of the sequences that visually indicate the authorization transaction sequence.

Figure 1-3 shows the agent sequence, in which an AAA server acts as the middleman between the client and the service equipment responsible for provisioning the client's request.

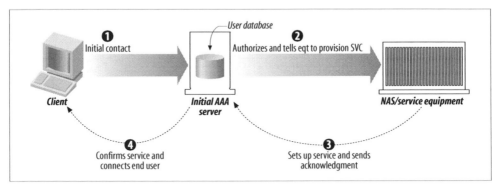

Figure 1-3. The agent sequence

Figure 1-4 shows the pull sequence, in which the user contacts the service equipment directly. The equipment then "pulls" an authorization from the AAA server.

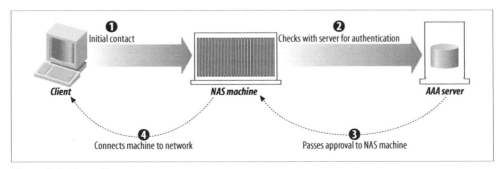

Figure 1-4. The pull sequence

Figure 1-5 shows the push sequence, in which the client system gets an authorization from the AAA server and then pushes it to the service equipment.

Roaming

To add an interesting twist to the progression, let's talk about roaming. The examples I've presented thus far assume that the service equipment and AAA server are all under the direct control and ownership of a single entity, the user's home organization (UHO). But what happens when the service equipment is owned and operated by another organization? This model is called *roaming*, and the Roaming Operations

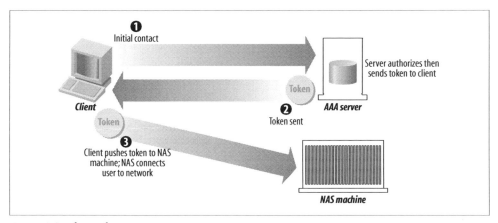

Figure 1-5. The push sequence

Working Group (Roamops) has been formed to explore this situation. Roaming is actually quite common: revisiting an earlier example, a user connecting to a set of dial-up ports that his ISP is renting from a larger service provider is roaming, since the service equipment is in another provider's domain.

The same combinations of authorization sequences—agent, push, and pull—are possible with roaming. Figures 1-6 through 1-8 depict typical roaming authorization sequences.

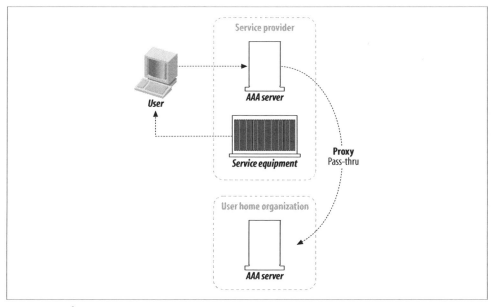

Figure 1-6. The roaming agent sequence

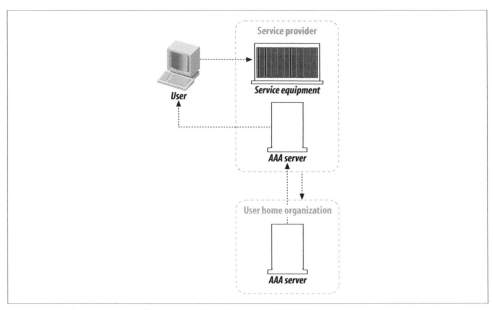

Figure 1-7. The roaming pull sequence

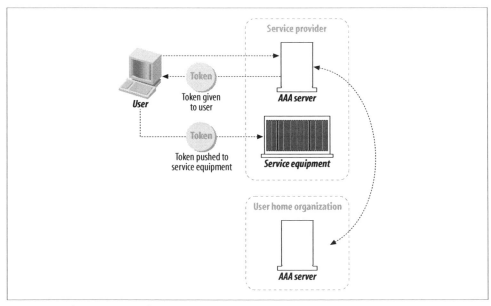

Figure 1-8. The roaming push sequence

Distributed Services

Now consider a situation in which a service provider contracts with numerous whole-salers to provide services to its user base. For example, a provider could guarantee a certain amount of bandwidth across the country for a particular company. The front-line ISP with which the company, as a client, contracts needs to set a QoS policy on equipment across the country to maintain its contractual duty to the customer. The customer, in this situation, is using a distributed service. Figure 1-9 illustrates this.

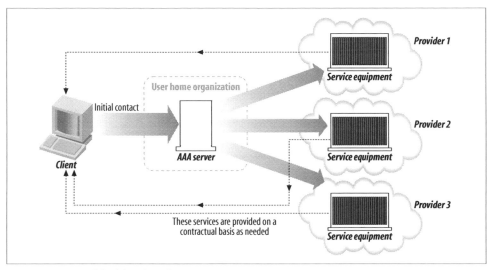

Figure 1-9. A model of distributed services

In Figure 1-9, we make the assumption that the user first contacts his UHO and gains authorization from its servers, which then provision his service from the other organizations involved in his contract. But this is not necessarily the case. The contacts between the equipment at the first and second organizations can use any of the three authorization sequences we described earlier. For instance, the user can contact the service equipment in the first hop, using the pull authorization sequence. Following that, the ISP's equipment will use a push sequence: it will contact the AAA server at the second organization, obtain authorization, and push the service equipment. This process can be carried out as many times as necessary to fulfill the front-line ISP's contractual obligations. Figure 1-10 demonstrates this type of distributed service that involves three different service-provider organizations.

These models open up possibilities for new features in protocols based around the AAA design. First, examine the possibility of an organization using a type of "credit" for another system. For example, the length and traffic of a certain route from Philadelphia to San Francisco could result in delays for AAA traffic being sent from the east coast ISP to the west coast ISP. The Philadelphia ISP equipment, knowing about the delays, could proceed and grant authorization ahead of time to the San Francisco equipment without having express authorization from the west coast provider. However, there needs to be a provision in whatever AAA-based protocol is used to revoke that authorization should either the west coast equipment deny the request

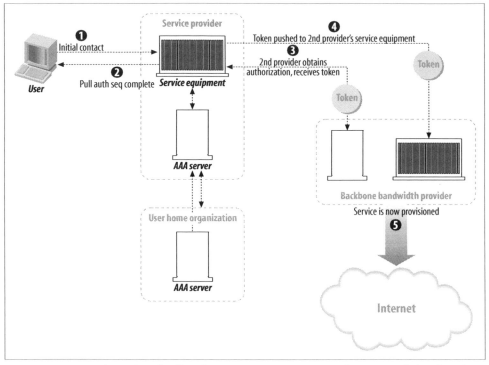

Figure 1-10. Using the push and pull authorization sequences to provide a user with distributed services

once it receives it, or the delays be so long that the response from the San Francisco equipment is lost.

As well, distributed services in concert with roaming can create entirely new business and IT infrastructure models. For example, an organization could exist solely to provide authentication and authorization functions to a variety of diverse networks. Such an "AAA broker" would be able to provide AAA services to ISP wholesalers, individual service providers, and corporations outsourcing their own dial-up pools. The various RFCs that make up the AAA design allow for such an organization to exist based on the capabilities they specify.

Policies

Policies, in short, are what an AAA server analyzes and uses to determine whether a request is valid and should be granted. Any server that meets the generic AAA requirements must have some way of storing and retrieving policy information. These policies are stored in a policy repository, which can be virtually anything that stores information: a database, a flat text file, or some other storage mechanism. The one key point about the policy repository in general is that it requires a unique namespace—the name of the server, to be simple—so that remote devices can query and make requests for that AAA server's resources.

The AAA framework provides for a policy set that spans across multiple domains and entities. It lists three specific tasks for an AAA server in terms of using policies: they must be retrieved, evaluated, and enforced. How this is done can vary greatly depending on the environment. It can even involve directory queries via an open-directory protocol, such as LDAP.

A great deal of work goes into policy evaluation. A simple dial-up user doesn't require much analysis on the part of the AAA server: it examines a rather simple policy, perhaps one that states whether the user is allowed to log on and then appropriately answers the request. However, authorization might also involve the provisioning of distributed services, and current status information could be vital in servicing the request. The AAA server might not have that information at hand, so it has to have a way to contact the appropriate resources, gather the information it needs, and then analyze that information against its policy.

Policies can also be distributed. In the previous example, let's say a user requires a 512 KB connection with no greater than three hops to a destination. The AAA server gathers the relevant information and authorizes the request, since it knows from its requests to the service equipment at each hop that traffic is light and there are ports and bandwidth available for the connection. The AAA server, having authorized the request, can then distribute a policy to the routers at each hop, ensuring the contractual QoS threshold. It can also set limits, via IP address restrictions, on where requests made over the connection can go.

Policy Framework Points

Some more terminology is required to understand how systems interact to use policies. RFC policies are retrieved using a policy retrieval point (PRP) from a policy repository. They are then evaluated at a policy decision point (PDP) and enforced at a policy enforcement point (PEP), or the target. The requests of other devices for information (like in the previous example) are made of policy information points (PIPs) and are queried and retrieved using policy information blocks (PIBs).

In general, AAA servers can be PRPs and PDPs, and various pieces of service equipment serve as PEPs. Policy repositories are present anywhere on the network, including various AAA servers or in dedicated database servers. In network designs involving distributed services, multiple service providers may have their own AAA equipment with their own policy repositories that can be queried using PIPs and PIBs.

The RFC requires that the "…AAA protocol…be able to transport both policy definitions and the information needed to evaluate policies. It must also support queries for policy information."

Resource and Session Management

The final components of the authorization framework (at least the final in terms of the scope of this book) are the specifications for resource and session management. The problem with covering this is that, so far, the RFC waxes theoretical much more than it offers concrete dimensions and mechanisms. But let's first look into what resource and session management are and how they can benefit a protocol that is based on the AAA model.

Resource management is basically the ability to monitor resources that have been previously allocated. A program or utility called the "resource manager" would be able to receive and display information on a resource in real time. Such a program could, for example, monitor a pool of dial-up ports on a terminal server and report information to the monitor program.

This is perhaps the simpler mechanism of the two to implement into a protocol, but there are inherent problems. With fewer AAA servers, there isn't much traffic involved in real-time monitoring, and the equipment is more likely to be confined to one entity's realm. Once the AAA server group expands and, particularly, begins to span multiple domains, it becomes increasingly problematic to maintain the identity of specific servers. Uniqueness of sessions is critical, and in addition, some method of combining session and resource information with a unique identifier is needed. As has been well documented in a variety of applications, network synchronization has its own problems as well, such as resource contentions and deadlocks.

Session management is the capability of a protocol or piece of equipment to notify an AAA server of a change in conditions, and more ideally, to modify an existing session. That session could be changed, put on hold, or terminated based on changing conditions recorded by the resource manager. Consider a connection based on a contract that offers a specific QoS threshold (2 MB, for example) during working hours and another based on traffic load during non-working hours. A session manager would use the information from the resource manager (which in this case would monitor the session time and traffic load) and dynamically alter the parameters of the session when the traffic load became heavier and the clock struck 5 P.M. It would then send a note back to the AAA servers at the UHO, allowing them to record accounting information that could help with later billing requirements.

The combination of resource and session management allows complicated policies to be implemented and provisioned with ease, even across a distributed policy platform. The agility to change based on varied conditions is the focus of more research and development on the part of the AAA Working Group. They face numerous problems in designing a model to incorporate these desires. For one, it's been difficult up to now to synchronize a session database with the real state of a session. Connection delays and packet losses all come into contention when real-time monitoring is used. Although there are commercial database products that claim to have solved this "inter-domain database replication problem," there is yet to be an official specification of this inside an RFC.

The significance of monitoring data and traffic can easily be seen when you consider the oft-referenced ISP wholesaler. He often makes agreements with providers to offer a certain number of ports for a certain length of time, say 1,000 ports in any of 10 locations from 7 A.M. to 9 P.M., and 650 ports in any of these locations from 9:01 P.M. to 6:59 A.M. With possibly 1,000 requests coming in at the same time (the dreaded "overload" factor capacity planners try to stifle) from 10 different locations, it would be crucial in the financial interests of both companies to ensure that only 1,000 ports (or 650 ports) were used. If monitoring was not used, it would be impossible for the wholesaler to determine that only 1,000 ports were used: that is to say, the ISP could exceed his allotment and the wholesaler would not be aware of it. This is especially bad if the wholesaler's modem:user ratio were particularly low, even 1:1, since any overage would result in a legitimate user from another organization being denied access.

As I mentioned earlier, the details and complications of resource and session management are far beyond what I intend to cover in this book. However, you should be aware of how the authorization framework and session management can be implemented and what the limitations are.

And Now, RADIUS

There's been much talk of AAA and so little of RADIUS. This is largely because RADIUS will not be eternally the access control protocol of choice. In fact, RADIUS was created by a separate working group long before the AAA design and fundamentals were brought to existence. The similarities are, however, remarkable.

AAA is the foundation of the next generation remote access protocol. Developments in creating the next protocol are being made as I write this, so the days of RADIUS being the standard aren't infinite. But on the same token, RADIUS has an established and well-respected presence in the industry, so it has a definite future.

A Brief History

RADIUS, like most innovative products, was built from a need. In this case, the need was to have a method of authenticating, authorizing, and accounting for users needing access to heterogeneous computing resources. Merit Networks, a big player in creating the Internet as we know it, operated a pool of dial-up resources across California. At the time, authentication methods were peculiar to specific pieces of equipment, which added a lot of overhead and didn't allow for much in the way of management flexibility and reporting. As the dial-up user group grew, the corporation realized they needed a mechanism more flexible and extensible than remaining with their proprietary, unwieldy equipment and scripts. Merit sent out a request for proposal, and Livingston Enterprises was one of the first respondents. Representatives for Merit and Livingston contacted each other, and after meeting at a conference, a very early version of RADIUS was written. More software was constructed to operate between the service equipment Livingston manufactured and the RADIUS server at Merit, which was operating with Unix. The developer of RADIUS, Steve Willins, still remains on the RFC document. From that point on, Livingston Enterprises became Lucent, and Merit and Lucent took the RADIUS protocol through the steps to formalization and industry acceptance. Both companies now offer a RADIUS server to the public at no charge.

Properties of RADIUS

The RFC specifications for the RADIUS protocol dictate that RADIUS:

- Is a UDP-based connectionless protocol that doesn't use direct connections
- Uses a hop-by-hop security model
- Is stateless (more to come on that later)
- Supports PAP and CHAP authentication via PPP
- Uses MD5 for password-hiding algorithms
- Provides over 50 attribute/value pairs with the ability to create vendor-specific pairs
- Supports the authentication–authorization–accounting model

In addition, RADIUS enjoys support by virtually every commercially available NAS product, ensuring its future well into the next 10 years.

Limitations of RADIUS

RADIUS, while having many positive attributes to its name, does have limitations. Doesn't everything, after all?

First, security is an obstacle in some implementations. Despite the irony, if an implementation in which there are several proxy RADIUS servers is used, all hops must view, perform logic on, and pass on all data in the request, hidden or not. This means that all data is available at every hop, which is not the most secure environment in which to place such sensitive data as certificates and passwords.

Second, RADIUS, at least in its most general incarnation, has no support for recalling and deallocating resources after an authorization has been issued. For instance, as mentioned earlier, it's possible to have a multi-hop proxy RADIUS chain in which the first server grants the request and subsequently contacts the necessary equipment to provision the services. If for some reason the service is not available (possibly because of a time-of-day restriction or an account suspension that the frontline RADIUS server isn't aware of), there is no provision in the RFC specification to deny and disconnect the service now that a rejection has been made. Some vendors have developed support for subsequent rejections—including knocking a user off at his specific time limit rather than just denying him access the next time he attempts to connect—but there's not a provision for this in the official specification.

Third, RADIUS is stateless (you heard about this earlier). That is to say, it does not keep track of configuration settings, transaction information, or any other data for the next session. When a program "does not maintain state" (is stateless) or when the infrastructure of a system prevents a program from maintaining state, it cannot take information about the last session into the next, such as settings the user made or conditions that arose during processing. In terms of using RADIUS, this complicates resource and session management solutions like I described previously.

And finally, users of RADIUS have noted that RADIUS has scalability problems. On the first page of the RFC is a note from the IESG: "Experience has shown that [RADIUS] can suffer degraded performance and lost data when used in large scale systems, in part because it does not include provisions for congestion control. Readers of this document may find it beneficial to track the progress of the IETF's AAA Working Group, which may develop a successor protocol that better addresses the scaling and congestion control issues."

If you were reading closely, you'd see that even the RADIUS RFC, itself, notes the fact that it's a limited protocol. Unfortunately, adding the complications of just some of the limitations I presented here can cause problems on a large-scale enterprise level. RADIUS is not always going to be the key authenticator protocol, but its basis on the AAA framework (and your familiarity with its underpinnings, because of this book) makes the transition from RADIUS to the next, more scalable protocol much easier.

So there's the overview of the key design aspects behind RADIUS. In the next chapter, I'll discuss RADIUS specifically and go through the RFC, explaining each part in detail.

## CHAPTER 2

RADIUS Specifics

In this chapter, I'll step through the most important sections of the RADIUS RFC and interpret them. Since the RFC is approximately 80 pages long, it's not appropriate to provide every detail here. Some portions of the document are antiquated, seldom used, or simply not important. While formality dictates their presence in the official document, this chapter is meant more as a working reference guide.

Using UDP versus TCP

A question frequently asked of the RADIUS development team is why the protocol uses the UDP protocol instead of TCP. For purely operational requirements, UDP was selected largely because RADIUS has a few inherent properties that are characteristic of UDP: RADIUS requires that failed queries to a primary authentication server be redirected to a secondary server, and to do this, a copy of the original request must exist above the transport layer of the OSI model. This, in effect, mandates the use of retransmission timers.

The protocol bets on the patience of users to wait for a response. It assumes some middle ground between lightning fast and slow as molasses. The RADIUS RFC describes it best: "At one extreme, RADIUS does not require a "responsive" detection of lost data. The user is willing to wait several seconds for the authentication to complete. The generally aggressive TCP retransmission (based on average round trip time) is not required, nor is the acknowledgment overhead of TCP. At the other extreme, the user is not willing to wait several minutes for authentication. Therefore the reliable delivery of TCP data two minutes later is not useful. The faster use of an alternate server allows the user to gain access before giving up."

Since RADIUS is stateless (as I mentioned in Chapter 1), UDP seems natural, as UDP is stateless, too. With TCP, clients and servers must have special code or administrative workarounds to mitigate the effects of power losses, reboots, heavy network traffic, and decommissioning of systems. UDP prevents this headache since it allows one session to open and remain open throughout the entire transaction.

To allow for heavy systems use and traffic on the backend, which can sometimes delay queries and look-ups by as much as 30 seconds or more, it was determined that RADIUS should be multithreaded. UDP allows RADIUS to spawn to serve multiple requests at a time, and each session has full, uninhibited communication abilities between the network gear and the client. Thus, UDP was a good fit.

The only downside to using UDP is that developers must create and manage retransmission timers themselves—this capability is built into TCP. However, the RADIUS group felt that this one downside was far outweighed by the convenience and simplicity of using UDP. And so it was.

Packet Formats

The RADIUS protocol uses UDP packets to pass transmissions between the client and server. The protocol communicates on port 1812, which is a change from the original RADIUS RFC document. The first revision specified that RADIUS communications were to take place on port 1645, but later this was found to conflict with the "Datametrics" service.

RADIUS uses a predictable packet structure to communicate, which is shown in Figure 2-1.

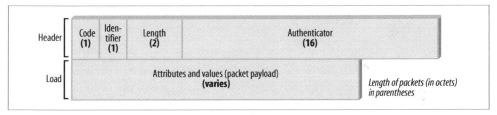

Figure 2-1. A depiction of the RADIUS data packet structure

The data structure is broken down into five distinct regions, which are discussed later in this chapter.

Code

The code region is one octet long and serves to distinguish the type of RADIUS message being sent in that packet. Packets with invalid code fields are thrown away without notification. Valid codes are:

1

> Access-Request

2

> Access-Accept

3

   Access-Reject

4

   Accounting-Request

5

   Accounting-Response

11

   Access-Challenge

12

   Status-Server (under continued development)

13

   Status-Client (under continued development)

255

   Reserved

Identifier

The identifier region is one octet long and is used to perform threading, or the automated linking of initial requests and subsequent replies. RADIUS servers can generally intercept duplicate messages by examining such factors as the source IP address, the source UDP port, the time span between the suspect messages, and the identifier field.

Length

The length region is two octets long and is used to specify how long a RADIUS message is. The value in this field is calculated by analyzing the code, identifier, length, authenticator, and attribute fields and finding their sum. The length field is checked when a RADIUS server receives a packet to ensure data integrity. Valid length values range between 20 and 4096.

The RFC specification requires certain behaviors of RADIUS servers with regard to incorrect length data. If the RADIUS server receives a transmission with a message longer than the length field, it ignores all data past the end point designated in the length field. Conversely, if the server receives a shorter message than the length field reports, the server will discard the message.

Authenticator

The authenticator region, often 16 octets long, is the field in which the integrity of the message's payload is inspected and verified. In this field, the most important octet is transmitted before any other—the value used to authenticate replies from the RADIUS server. This value is also used in the mechanism to conceal passwords.

There are two specific types of authenticator values: the request and response values. *Request authenticators* are used with `Access-Request` and `Accounting-Request` packets. In the request value, the field is 16 octets long and is generated on a completely random basis so as to thwart any attacks. While RADIUS doesn't make a provision for protecting communication against wiretapping and packet capture, random values coupled with a strong password make attacking and snooping difficult.

The *response authenticator* is used in `Access-Accept`, `Access-Reject`, and `Access-Challenge` packets. The value is calculated using a one-way MD5 hash generated from the values of the code, identifier, length, and request-authenticator regions of the packet header, followed by the packet payload and the shared secret. (I'll cover shared secrets in detail later in this chapter.) Example 2-1 shows an equation to represent how this hash is computed.

Example 2-1. From RFC 2865, the MD5 hash for the response authenticator header field

```
ResponseAuth = MD5(Code+ID+Length+RequestAuth+Attributes+Secret)
```

Packet Types

At this point, we have covered the structure of the packets RADIUS uses to transmit data. But what do these packets do? There are four RADIUS packet types that are relevant to the authentication and authorization phases of the AAA transaction:

```
Access-Request
Access-Accept
Access-Reject
Access-Challenge
```

While the accounting packet types are covered in detail in Chapter 4, the next section will step through these packets and detail their intent, format, and structure.

Access-Request

Packet Type	Request
Code	1
Identifier	Unique per request
Length	Header length plus all additional attribute data
Authenticator	Request
Attribute Data	2 or more

The `Access-Request` packet is used by the service consumer when it is requesting a particular service from a network. The client sends a Request packet to the RADIUS server with a list of the requested services. The key factor in this transmission is the code field in the packet header: it must be set to 1, the unique value of the Request packet. The RFC states that replies must be sent to all valid Request packets, whether the reply is an authorization or a rejection.

The payload of the Access-Request packet should include the username attribute to identify the person attempting to gain access to the network resource. The payload is required to contain the IP address or canonical name of the network equipment from which it is requesting service. It also has to contain a user password, a CHAP-based password, or a state identifier, but not both types of passwords. The user password must be hashed using MD5.

How do these rules apply to RADIUS proxy chains? Basically, new packets need to be created whenever attributes are changed, since identifying information is changed. Attributes with shared secrets, which are covered in detail later in this chapter, need to be reversed by the proxy server (to obtain the original payload information) and then encrypted again with the secret that the proxy server shares with the remote server.

The Access-Request packet structure is shown in Figure 2-2.

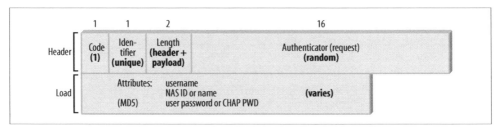

Figure 2-2. A typical Access-Request packet

Access-Accept

Packet Type	Response
Code	2
Identifier	Identical to Access-Request per transaction
Length	Header length plus all additional attribute data
Authenticator	Response
Attribute Data	0 or more

The Access-Accept packets are sent by the RADIUS server to the client to acknowledge that the client's request is granted. If all of the requests in the Access-Request payload are acceptable, then the RADIUS server must set the response packet's code field to 2. The client, upon receiving the accept packet, matches it up with the response packet by using the identifier field. Packets not following this standard are discarded.

Of course, to ensure that the request and accept packets are matched up—that is to say, to make sure the accept response is sent in reply to the respective request packet—the identifier field in the Access-Accept packet header must contain an identical value to that of the Access-Request field.

The Access-Accept packet can contain as much or as little attribute information as it needs to include. Most likely the attribute information in this packet will describe the types of services that have been authenticated and authorized so that the client can then set itself up to use those services. However, if no attribute information is included, the client assumes that the services it requested are the ones granted.

The Access-Accept packet structure is shown in Figure 2-3.

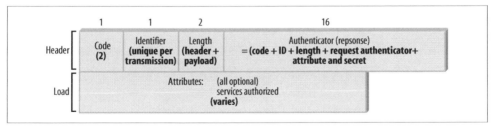

Figure 2-3. A typical Access-Accept packet

Access-Reject

Packet Type	Response
Code	3
Identifier	Identical to Access-Request
Length	Header length plus all additional attribute data
Authenticator	Response
Attribute Data	0 or more

The RADIUS server is required to send an Access-Reject packet back to the client if it must deny any of the services requested in the Access-Request packet. The denial can be based on system policies, insufficient privileges, or any other criteria—this is largely a function of the individual implementation. The Access-Reject can be sent *at any time* during a session, which makes them ideal for enforcing connection time limits. However, not all equipment supports receiving the Access-Reject during a pre-established connection.

The payload for this packet type is limited to two specific attributes: the Reply-Message and Proxy-State attributes. While these attributes can appear more than once inside the payload of the packet, apart from any vendor-specific attributes, no other attributes are allowed, under the RFC specification, to be included in the packet. (Vendor-specific attributes are covered in detail both later in this chapter and throughout the remainder of the book.)

The Access-Reject packet structure is shown in Figure 2-4.

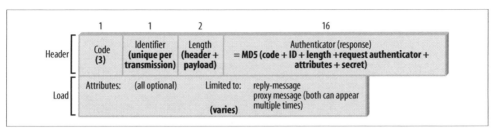

Figure 2-4. A typical Access-Reject packet

Access-Challenge

Packet Type	Response
Code	11
Identifier	Identical to Access-Request
Length	Header length plus all additional attribute data
Authenticator	Response
Attribute Data	0 or more

If a server receives conflicting information from a user, requires more information, or simply wishes to decrease the risk of a fraudulent authentication, it can issue an Access-Challenge packet to the client. The client, upon receipt of the Access-Challenge packet, must then issue a new Access-Request with the appropriate information included.

It should be noted that some clients don't support the challenge/response process like this; in that case, the client treats the Access-Challenge packet as an Access-Reject packet. Some clients, however, do support challenging, and at that point a message can be given to the user at the client requesting the additional authentication information—it's not necessary in that situation to set off another round of request/response packets.

Much like the Access-Reject packet, there are only two standard attributes that can be included in an Access-Challenge packet: the State and Reply-Message attributes. Any necessary vendor-specific attributes can be included as well. The Reply-Message attribute can be included in the packet multiple times, but the State attribute is limited to a single instance. The State attribute is copied unchanged into the Access-Request that is returned to the challenging server.

The Access-Challenge packet structure is shown in Figure 2-5.

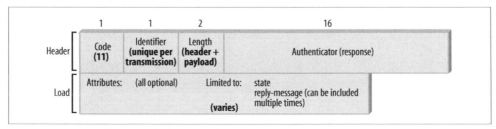

Figure 2-5. A typical Access-Challenge packet

Shared Secrets

To strengthen security and increase transactional integrity, the RADIUS protocol uses the concept of shared secrets. Shared secrets are values generated at random that are known to both the client and the server (hence the "shared"). The shared secret is used within all operations that require hiding data and concealing values. The only technical limitation is that shared secrets must be greater than 0 in length, but the RFC recommends that the secret be at least 16 octets. A secret of that length is virtually impossible to crack with brute force. The same set of best practices that dictate password usage also govern the proper use of RADIUS shared secrets.

Shared secrets (commonly called just "secrets") are unique to a particular RADIUS client and server pair. For instance, if an end user subscribes to multiple Internet service providers for his dial-up access, he indirectly makes requests to multiple RADIUS servers. The shared secrets between the client NAS equipment in ISPs A, B, and C that are used to communicate with the respective RADIUS servers should not match.

While some larger scale RADIUS implementations may believe that protecting transactional security by using an automated shared-secret changer is a prudent move, there is a rather large pitfall: there is no guarantee the clients and servers can synchronize to the new shared secret at the most appropriate time. And even if it was certain that the simultaneous synchronization could occur, if there are outstanding requests to the RADIUS server and the client is busy processing (and, therefore, it misses the cue to synchronize the new secret), then those outstanding requests will be rejected by the server. The situation would be tantamount to having your checking account numbers stolen: when the bank gives you new account numbers, outstanding checks written on your old account will bounce since that account was closed.

Attributes and Values

Although at this point the attribute field in a RADIUS packet may seem like nothing more than a glorified way to determine header information, there's a lot more going on than meets the eye. Specifically, the entire RADIUS transaction is built around passing to and from the client and server attribute-value pairs (AVPs) that contain virtually every property and characteristic of the AAA transaction.

To enhance security, the RADIUS RFC restricts some attributes from being sent in certain packets—or to be more specific, the timing of certain packets. For instance, to prevent the password from ever crossing the wire more than once for one authentication/authorization process, the User-Password attribute is never allowed to be sent in a reply packet from the server to the client. Even more stringently, the RFC prevents some attributes from even being present in certain transactions, while others can appear more than once, and still others only once. More information on restrictions like these is presented in the sections that follow.

Attributes in a packet all follow a specific field format. From this point on, I'll refer to this field format as:

Attribute Number
> This number denotes the type of attribute presented in the packet. The attribute's name is not passed in the packet—just the number. Generally, attribute numbers can range from 1–255, with one specific number serving as a "gateway" of sorts for vendors to provide their own specific attributes.

Attribute Length
> This field describes the length of the attribute field, which must be three or greater. It behaves in much the same way as the length field of the RADIUS packet header.

Value
> Containing the property or characteristic of the attribute itself, this field is required for each attribute presented, even if the value itself is null. The length of this will vary based on the inherent nature of the attribute itself.

The concepts of attributes and values themselves are worthy of a bit more discussion.

Attributes

Attributes simply describe a behavior or a property of a type of service. While most attributes are included to denote a particular setting for a service type, the presence of some attributes in the packet tells the RADIUS server what it needs to know. As you'll see later in this chapter, the very inclusion of the CHAP-Password attribute in a packet signals to the RADIUS server the proper hashings and password-concealing processes to perform for that particular transaction. This is a unique property of attributes—they can stand alone, while values simply cannot.

Attributes are transmitted inside the RADIUS packet in a predetermined, standard format, as shown in Figure 2-6.

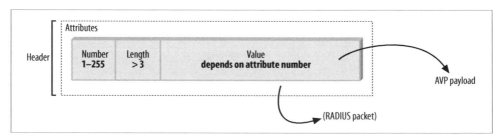

Figure 2-6. The standard AVP transmission pattern

The AVP structure shown in Figure 2-6 consists of a continuous set of bytes containing at least three octets, with the first octet being the type, the second the length, and the final octet the value of the attribute itself.

The RADIUS server knows enough about an attribute that its official name need not be transmitted in the packet. The code number (the attribute number) is enough to deduce the kind of information being transmitted in that particular value. Note that while there is an official guide to all of the attribute names in the RFC, these aren't required, and some vendors may modify the diction of the names in their specific implementations.

Attribute types

The RADIUS implementation, according to the RFC, is designed to look for certain types of values in the value field of a particular attribute. For example, you wouldn't want random numbers in an attribute designed to pass a date, nor would you expect to have an IP address (consisting of numbers) in a random character string. To ease the confusion surrounding multiple attribute values being passed in one transaction, each attribute's corresponding value has been assigned a certain type. This simply describes what the value is—a number, an IP address, a date, and so on. There are six types as outlined in the RFC:

Integer (INT)
> Integer types are values that contain whole numbers, which are read "as they come." An attribute like `Idle-Timeout` might be set to the integer value of 15.

Enumerated (ENUM)
> Data that is of the enumerated type consists of an integer, but the value is based on a user-configurable set of range values and meanings. You may encounter enumerated values called *semantic integer values*, whereas *non-semantic integer values* are simply integer types. There will be more information later in this chapter about ENUM values.

IP Address (IPADDR)
> This data type is a 32-bit number designed to pass a correctly formed IP address. While RADIUS by default looks at an IP address at face value, some implementations can be configured to handle it with a preconfigured value, such as a particular subnet mask. Also, a recent extension to the RADIUS protocol allows IPv6 addresses to be used in this type. Much of the handling of this data type is left up to the implementation and operating environment.

Character String (STRING)
> Character strings are generally defined to be UTF-8 printable strings that can be read at face value. The data is passed as a character array that can be bounded or unbounded, whichever is appropriate. The RADIUS RFC has specific notes regarding handling character arrays (particularly with printing issues) that are beyond the scope of this discussion.

Date (DATE)
> The date type is a 32-bit unsigned number representing elapsed seconds since January 1, 1970.

Binary (BINARY)
> Often peculiar to an implementation, binary values ("0" or "1") are read at face value.

The all-caps notations contained in the parentheses beside each term heading indicate the proper notational abbreviation for each of the attribute types.

Vendor-specific attributes

As with most of the RADIUS protocol, there is much flexibility for vendor-specific attribute types to come about in different implementations. Much of this is created to directly support special, non-standard or value-added features that some particular RADIUS client equipment is capable of provisioning. Of course, presumably because there in fact *is* a standard, some vendors—notably US Robotics/3Com—do not follow the RFC specification.

As mentioned earlier in this chapter, the RADIUS protocol defines a particular AVP as a "gateway" AVP in which vendor-specific attributes, or VSAs, can be encapsulated. The VSA is carried in value payload of the standard AVP 26, called Vendor-Specific. Figure 2-7 shows the standard AVP and how the VSA information is carried within.

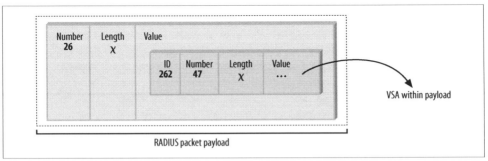

Figure 2-7. The passing of a VSA within a standard AVP

In Figure 2-7, the four standard parts of any VSA can be distinguished: the vendor ID, the vendor type, the length, and the value.

Vendor ID

> This section of the VSA contains four octets that represent the VSA's developer/designer/owner. These standard codes are defined in the RFC 1700 document as "Assigned Numbers." More specifically, the individual vendors are coded with unique numbers called Network Management Private Enterprise Codes, or NMPECs.
>
> The order of the vendor ID field contents is based on a stringent standard, with the highest-order byte of the four-octet value being set to zero, and then the last three bytes set to the NMPEC code as described previously. The whole lot is then converted into the portable byte format known as "network byte ordering." (A discussion of network byte ordering is beyond the scope of this chapter. A web search engine can turn up detailed information and history on this if you wish.)

Vendor type

> The vendor type field, which is one octet in length, functionally behaves in much the same way as the attribute number in a standard AVP. Vendor types are values with a range between 1 and 255, and the significance and meaning of each of the values is known to the vendor-specific logic inside the RADIUS server.

Length

> This field is a one-octet number that indicates the length of the entire VSA, with the minimum length of the entire VSA being seven. Again, the behavior of this field is similar to the length field in a standard, RFC-defined AVP.

Value

> The value field is required to be at least one octet in length and contains data that is specific to the VSA itself. Most of these values are read, interpreted, and analyzed by RADIUS clients and servers on the receiving end that are aware of the special features and non-standard abilities that their particular implementations support.

Values

Recall that all attributes must have values, even if the value of the attribute is null. Values represent the information that each particular attribute was designed to convey. They carry the "meat" of the information. Values must conform to the attribute type rules outlined previously. Table 2-1 shows examples of each attribute type and the expected value field payload for each.

Table 2-1. Attribute types and value field payloads

Attribute type	Length (in octets)	Size/Range	Example payloads
Integer (INT)	4	32-bit unsigned	6 256 2432 65536
Enumerated (ENUM)	4	32-bit unsigned	3 = Callback-Login 4 = Callback-Framed 13 = Framed-Compression 26 = Vendor-Specific
String (STRING)	1–253	Variable	"Charlotte" "Raleigh" "206.229.254.2" "aslyterdesign.com"
IP Address (IPADDR)	4	32-bit	0xFFFFFE 0xC0A80102 0x1954FF8E 0x00000A
Date (DATE)	4	32-bit unsigned	0xC0A80102 0xFFFFFE 0x00000A 0x1954FF8E
Binary (BINARY)	1	1 bit	1

Each of these value properties is enumerated (pun intended) and explained in the RADIUS RFC.

Dictionaries

The RADIUS server machines must have a way of relating which attribute corresponds to which attribute number and expected type. It also must be aware of any vendor-specific attributes it must support to contact the RADIUS client equipment that is operating in the same environment. Much like a dictionary of the English language contains words, their word types (verb, noun, preposition, etc.), and their definitions, a RADIUS dictionary keeps track of the properties of all standard and the appropriate vendor-specific attributes.

The commonly found RADIUS flexibility is extended to the dictionary implementation. Dictionaries can be stored in flat text files, in databases, or by just about any other means—the only constraint here is the accessibility of the information to the RADIUS server. While more exotic means of storing the file are not out of the question, experience shows that by far the two most common methods of storing the dictionary information are in text files and databases.

Here is an excerpt of a common flat text file dictionary:

```
#   ATTRIBUTE-NAME          TYPE
#-------------------------------------
1   User-Name               STRING
2   User-Password           STRING
3   CHAP-Password           STRING
4   NAS-IP-Address          IPADDR
5   NAS-Port                INT
6   Service-Type            ENUM
7   Framed-Protocol         ENUM
8   Framed-IP-Address       IPADDR
9   Framed-IP-Netmask       IPADDR
10  Framed-Routing          ENUM
```

 Earlier in this chapter, I said that RADIUS implementations have enough information so that the text name of each attribute doesn't need to be transmitted. Most dictionary files *do* include this information for the sake of the administrator—it's difficult to edit a file based solely on numbers, and in the name of convenience, the full name is included. The full name is *not* transmitted in a packet.

Recall from the discussion of attribute types earlier that a special type of integer value, the enumerated (ENUM) type, is simply a set of integers whose values are of different significance based on the specific attribute. For instance, in the previous example, the Framed-Protocol attribute is of the enumerated type; thus, the RADIUS server will need to know the meanings of the different values the Framed-Protocol attribute will pass. Consider this next example, which shows the way a RADIUS server would account for the different meanings of the enumerated values for the Framed-Protocol attribute:

```
# VALUE-MEANING                        FOR ATTRIBUTE
#-------------------------------------------------
1 PPP                                  7
2 SLIP                                 7
3 AppleTalk Rem. Acc. Protocol (ARAP)  7
4 Gandalf SingleLink/MultiLink         7
5 Xylogics proprietary IPX/SLIP        7
6 X.75 Synchronous                     7
```

Each RADIUS implementation may store information about any vendor-specific attributes in a dictionary as well. The format of a flat text file dictionary complete with vendor-specific attributes would look similar, except the vendor ID code (based from the NMPEC code) must be included as well.

Authentication Methods

RADIUS supports a variety of different protocol mechanisms to transmit sensitive user-specific data to and from the authentication server. The two most common are the Password Authentication Protocol (PAP) and the CHAP. RADIUS also allows for more attributes and methods developed by vendors, including support for features peculiar to Windows NT, Windows 2000, and other popular network operating systems and directory services. The following section explores the two most common methods in greater detail.

PAP

The User-Password attribute in a requesting packet signals to the RADIUS server that the PAP protocol will be used for that transaction. It's important to note that the only mandatory field in this case is the User-Password field. The User-Name field does not have to be included in the requesting packet, and it's entirely possible that a RADIUS server along a proxy chain will change the value in the User-Name field.

The algorithm used to hide the original user's password is composed of many elements. First, the client detects the identifier and the shared secret for the original request and submits it to an MD5 hashing sequence. The client's original password is put through the XOR process and the result coming from these two sequences is then put in the User-Password field. The receiving RADIUS server then reverses these procedures to determine whether to authorize the connection. The very nature of the password-hiding mechanism prevents a user from determining if, when the authentication fails, the failure was caused by an incorrect password or an invalid secret. Most commercial RADIUS servers, though, include logic that looks at the series of packets previously transmitted from the same client. If a number passes through the connection correctly, most likely the few packets that failed did so because of an incorrect password.

CHAP

CHAP is based on the premise that the password should never be sent in any packet across a network. CHAP dynamically encrypts the requesting user's ID and password. The user's machine then goes through its logon procedure, having obtained a key from the RADIUS client equipment of at least 16 octets in length. The client then hashes that key and sends back a CHAP ID, a CHAP response, and the username to the RADIUS client. The RADIUS client, having received all of the above, places the CHAP ID field into the appropriate places in the CHAP-Password attribute and then sends a response. The challenge value originally obtained is placed in either the CHAP-Challenge attribute or in the authenticator field in the header—this is so the server can easily access the value in order to authenticate the user.

To authenticate the user, the RADIUS server uses the CHAP-Challenge value, the CHAP ID, and the password on record for that particular user and submits it to another MD5 hashing algorithm. The result of this algorithm should be identical to the value found in the CHAP-Password attribute. If it's not, the server must deny the request; otherwise, the request is granted.

The fact that the password in a CHAP transaction is never passed across the network is just one reason why CHAP is an appealing authentication protocol. How does this work? The user data against which the hashing routine is run returns a one-way value that does not contain the password. So the server must have the current user's password stored in clear text in its own records in order to create a hash with which to compare. CHAP IDs are also non-persistent, which reduces the possibility of a third party sniffing or otherwise intruding on the transaction. Additionally, the CHAP protocol supports challenging the client anytime during the user's session, which increases the likelihood that invalid users are kept out of the system.

Using Strong, Secure Passwords

The security of CHAP and the integrity of transactions initiated using CHAP depends heavily on the strength of the user's password. In PAP authentication, the shared secret is used in conjunction with the MD5 hash to conceal the password. The actual password is used in much the same way with CHAP authentication. Despite the fact that the password itself is never transmitted, a weak, easily guessable password is fodder for crackers. This is because the values submitted to the MD5 hashing algorithm can be easily replicated or "backtracked."

Good passwords use words or phrases that can't be easily guessed, that aren't found in a dictionary, and that are of a length to make brute-force cracking impractical or impossible. To use passwords that don't meet these criteria is to place in jeopardy the security and integrity of the entire CHAP authentication mechanism itself.

Selecting PAP, CHAP, or Other Protocols

There is a school of thought on either side of using CHAP or PAP in a network that requires authorization. Some systems administrators think that because CHAP's security cannot be enforced when authorization requests must travel outside their realm of control, PAP is a more appropriate method. This is because with PAP, the strength of the shared secret used in the transmissions between the machines is under the direct control of the original administrator. As well, any particular administrator cannot be guaranteed that one authentication protocol will be used throughout any environment in which requests are passed through a proxy chain. In this case, the final authorizing sequence decides the authentication protocol.

RADIUS isn't limited at all to PAP or CHAP authentication. The limits on authenticator protocols are inherent to the operating system. For instance, RADIUS can support a domain attribute when logging into a Windows NT or Windows 2000 system. The key factor in supporting RADIUS authentication is that the password be available somehow to the host system. The most common way to do this is to use a Unix password file, but that particular file only works with PAP authentication. Passwords can also be retrieved from a directory service (such as Microsoft's Active Directory, Novell's eDirectory, or a generic LDAP directory store), from an encrypted file, or by some other means. All of this is to say that support for various authenticator protocols depends entirely on the configuration of a particular RADIUS environment.

Realms

While RADIUS can be as ignorant of externalities as an administrator wants, it can also be made aware of various implementations. RADIUS is flexible with regard to various design schemes to allow it to support different business and infrastructure models. Take, for instance, a cooperative agreement among three regional Internet service providers. Let's explore this example in greater detail.

Northwest Internet serves the northern and western portions of a state. Southeast Internet serves the southern and eastern regions, and Central State Internet provides support to the central area of a state. While each of these ISPs may have modem-pool resources in overlapping geographical areas, most of the access resources are confined to particular regions.

Now, each of the service providers determine that there is sufficient demand to offer a roaming service to customers to allow them to dial a local number anywhere in the state to access the Internet. While the service would be more expensive than normal, with a home-area dial-up service, a local number allows the customer to avoid expensive long-distance charges most hotels and other lodging establishments levy. Each ISP determines that it's not fiscally efficient for them to construct points of presence in each region, so they form a cooperative alliance in which each ISP allows the other two ISPs to have access to their respective modem pools. So Northwest Internet can offer a roaming service to its mobile users who happen to dial up in the southern and eastern portions of the state, and so on.

The key question here revolves around how each ISP can offer access and ensure that only valid users can connect to their resources, while protecting the sanctity and security of the respective providers' sensitive customer information. To fill this need, RADIUS comes with support for identifying users based on discrete design-based areas, or realms. *Realms* are identifiers that are placed before or after the values normally contained in the User-Name attribute that a RADIUS server can use to identify which server to contact to start the AAA process.

The first type of realm identifier is known as the prefix realm, in which the realm name is placed before the username, and the two are separated by a preconfigured character, most commonly @, \, or /. For instance, a user named *jhassell* who subscribes to Central State Internet's service (whose realm name is CSI) would configure his client to pass a username like *CSI\jhassell*.

The other realm identifier syntax is the suffix realm, where the username is placed before the realm name. The common separators are still used in this syntax as well, though by far the most common is the @ sign. For example, the user *awatson* subscribing to Northwest Internet's service (realm name: NWI) using realm suffix identification would pass a username like *awatson@NWI*.

RADIUS Hints

An administrator can configure a RADIUS server to grant some services by default to any authenticated user, while other configurations might permit only the services requested in the client's request packet to be authorized. RADIUS can be set up to handle service authorizations in countless different ways. The RADIUS RFC thus specifies information that can be included in a RADIUS packet header sent from a client to a server that "hints" to the server which explicit services it wants. These bits of information are called RADIUS hints.

RADIUS hints behave differently based on the way an administrator sets up his RADIUS client gear to authorize transactions. The RFC states that the receiving RADIUS server can choose whether to grant the hints requests if doing so would not violate the local security setup. If the RADIUS server chooses not to grant the hints request, though, it is also allowed under the RFC specification to authorize a service that can be granted based on the user's access policy. If it can't do this, then it must terminate and disconnect the session.

Hints are designed primarily for environments in which the RADIUS server has partial control of the resources needed to provision service for the client. For instance, the client may request a specific, static IP as paid for in her monthly billing by sending a hint in the request. The NAS gear, having obtained explicit authorization from the RADIUS server (eliminating the extra transaction hop to obtain authorization from the IP leasing pool machine), may then grant the request by telling the RADIUS server to send the details in an Access-Accept packet, alter the routing tables, and do whatever else needs done to provision the service.

It's important to note that RADIUS hints never have any effect on the base RADIUS protocol. They're simply small notes "under the table" to the RADIUS server from the client, requesting that the service have optional, temporary, or extra characteristics or abilities.

## CHAPTER 3

Standard RADIUS Attributes

In this chapter, I'll look at the global set of standard RADIUS attributes as per the RADIUS RFC. There are 63 attributes defined in the RFC that provide support and configuration options for everything from connection type, virtual terminals, and connect/session time limits to packet filtering and caller-return services. This chapter presents these attributes in alphabetical order.

One note: this chapter covers only the attributes based on the authentication and authorization processes of a RADIUS transaction, which are attributes 1–39 and 60–63. Attributes 40–59 are covered in Chapter 4.

Attribute Properties

Each attribute in this chapter is presented as a separate "nugget" of information. Each nugget contains a quick-reference chart for the particulars of the attribute, followed by a discussion of the attribute, where I discuss any special considerations in the usage or configuration of the attribute, how its use affects or requires other attributes, practical applications of the attribute, and how it sometimes differs from the theoretical implication from the RFC.

The Appendix contains a chart with all of the global standard RADIUS attributes (including those specific to accounting) and their numbers, lengths, values, and packet presence requirements.

Chapter 9 presents the attributes introduced and revised in the new RADIUS Extensions RFCs. I have separated these attributes to maintain the distinction exhibited in the RFCs.

Callback-ID

Attribute Number	20
Length	3 or more octets

Value	STRING
Allowed in	Access-Accept
Prohibited in	Access-Request, Access-Reject, Access-Challenge
Presence in Packet	Not required
Maximum Iterations	1

This attribute is used when a RADIUS implementation is set up to return a user's call. This is commonly used in corporate situations to avoid long-distance charges in hotel rooms and other remote locations. This value, a STRING, is often the identifier for a profile configured on the service equipment; there is no specific standard for a string name, a triggered action, or something else. In other words, it is environment-specific. RADIUS client gear is allowed to reject a connection if this attribute is present but not supported by that gear.

Callback-Number

Attribute Number	19
Length	3 or more octets
Value	STRING
Allowed in	Access-Request, Access-Accept
Prohibited in	Access-Reject, Access-Challenge
Presence in Packet	Not required
Maximum Iterations	1

The value of this attribute is the number to which the RADIUS client gear should return a call to the authenticating user. Depending on what packet this attribute is found in, different actions may be configured. For instance, if Callback-Number is found in an Access-Request packet, the implementation may assume that the end user is requesting callback service. If the attribute is found in the Access-Accept packet, it can mean anything that the administrator configuring the gear wants it to mean. In fact, in some cases, Callback-ID and Callback-Number will *not* be found together in one packet.

Coupled with the Callback-ID attribute, this attribute is one of several RADIUS security measures. In addition to being more convenient and cost-effective for companies with employees in hotels needing access to corporate IT resources, the callback mechanism is also a security device. The implementation could be configured to call a certain number when a certain username requests access. This way, if a hacker is located somewhere other than where the genuine user normally connects from, the hacker would not be able to authenticate.

Called-Station-ID

Attribute Number	30
Length	3 or more octets
Value	STRING
Allowed in	Access-Request

Prohibited in	Access-Accept, Access-Reject, Access-Challenge
Presence in Packet	Not required
Maximum Iterations	1

The value in this packet can tell the NAS gear what number the user dialed to gain access to its service. Using the Dialed Number Identification Service (DNIS), the NAS gear may use this data to authenticate based on location (if each point of presence in various locations has a different number). Also, the Called-Station-ID can be used to identify which RADIUS proxy server forwarded the request. Using this attribute in that manner is called "numbered-realm proxying."

Outside of standard dial-up Internet access, the Called-Station-ID attribute can be used in other applications. For example, in the publicly available wireless access industry, typically you will find the MAC address of the access point to which the wireless card is connected in this field, with the octets separated by hyphens. While this is certainly not a prescribed standard by any RFC, this is a best practice.

Calling-Station-ID

Attribute Number	31
Length	3 or more octets
Value	STRING
Allowed in	Access-Request
Prohibited in	Access-Accept, Access-Reject, Access-Challenge
Presence in Packet	Not required
Maximum Iterations	1

This attribute, in effect, is the NAS gear's Caller ID function. The value in this attribute carries the number of the calling party inside an Access-Request packet. This can be used both for convenience and security purposes. For instance, different access-control lists can be created, only allowing callers from certain places to be authenticated. As well, a regional POP could be managed and limited by only allowing callers from certain area codes and exchanges. This attribute could also be used in conjunction with a callback service. Much of the configuration of what the NAS gear does with the Calling-Station-ID attribute is environment specific; there is no standard manner to handle the attribute.

CHAP-Challenge

Attribute Number	60
Length	7 or more octets
Value	STRING
Allowed in	Access-Request
Prohibited in	Access-Accept, Access-Reject, Access-Challenge
Presence in Packet	Not required
Maximum Iterations	1

If a CHAP transaction is involved—in other words, if CHAP responses are requested from or required by the RADIUS client—then the original CHAP challenge is placed in the value field of this attribute. The CHAP request is then sent to another server, which attempts to authenticate the request based on the CHAP-Challenge value. Normally, these values are around 16 bytes, which allows the RADIUS client the option of using the value in this attribute as the request authenticator. The large allowable size of the value makes the attribute secure enough to allow this.

CHAP-Password

Attribute Number	3
Length	19
Value	STRING
Allowed in	Access-Request
Prohibited in	Access-Accept, Access-Reject, Access-Challenge
Presence in Packet	Required, unless User-Password is present
Maximum Iterations	1

CHAP-Password indicates to the RADIUS client gear that CHAP, instead of PAP, is going to be used for the transaction.

Of particular interest regarding CHAP-Password is the structure of the attribute, which is different than most of the other attributes. The CHAP-Password attribute is structured much like the vendor-specific AVP passed within the standard Vendor-Specific attribute, number 26. This abnormal structure is due to the additional data collected in a CHAP transaction that needs to be passed between the two parties. Let's take a closer look.

The CHAP identifier, a one-octet value that the RADIUS client gear assigned, is placed in the first octet of the attribute's value field. The response, effectively the CHAP password, completes the rest of the value field.

The RADIUS RFC requires that the User-Password and the CHAP-Password attributes be mutually exclusive, but one or the other is required in any transaction at all times.

How does the CHAP-Password attribute affect the RADIUS transaction? The sequence is this: a dial-up client connects to an ISP's NAS gear, which in turn issues a CHAP ID and sends it back to the client. The client generates a response to this challenge and places the response in the password section of the value field. The entire lot is then returned to the NAS gear. The NAS gear is relatively flexible in dealing with the challenge: if the challenge generated at the client side is 16 octets, it can be placed in the request authenticator *or* in the challenge section of the value field.

In either case, once the NAS gear receives the CHAP ID and CHAP password back from the client, it uses a hash computed from information in the Access-Request packet combined with the user's recorded password to construct a CHAP-Response, which is then compared with the information provided in this attribute. Matches result in a successful authentication; mismatches trigger an Access-Reject packet.

Class

Attribute Number	25
Length	3 or more octets
Value	STRING
Allowed in	Access-Accept
Prohibited in	Access-Request, Access-Reject, Access-Challenge
Presence in Packet	Not required
Maximum Iterations	Unlimited

The Class attribute mainly exists to funnel identification and property information to the accounting systems of RADIUS implementations. The RFC mandates that the Class attribute is completely and totally vendor and implementation specific, and also dictates that the RADIUS client not even *attempt* to act on or interpret the information stored within that attribute.

While the value of this attribute is a string, the RFC dictates that the gear treat the value of that string is a contiguous set of data, or a set of "undistinguished octets." That is to say, the RADIUS client must not expect any boundaries or spaces in the data.

Effectively, this attribute mainly groups and "classifies" connection information. Accounting data is often used to predict demand, determine load, and plan for the future. Although categorized information may be of no use at the present, when the only concern is authenticating, it may prove useful down the road to accounting users.

Filter-ID

Attribute Number	11
Length	3 or more octets
Value	STRING
Allowed in	Access-Accept
Prohibited in	Access-Request, Access-Reject, Access-Challenge
Presence in Packet	Not required
Maximum Iterations	Unlimited

Filter-ID is arguably one of the most pragmatic, useful attributes in the RADIUS specification. Filter-ID is based upon the common practice of packet filtering, the use of which is most often found in firewalls and intrusion detection systems. The premise behind packet filtering is to inspect each and every packet in a transaction or data stream in order to determine, based on rules that an administrator configures, whether those packets should be allowed to pass through.

In RADIUS, however, that use is not as distinct. The most parallel example of packet inspection as a security device is when you view the RADIUS client gear as a gateway. Indeed, the RADIUS client is the first hop on the packet's destination to the Internet, and the client can filter based on rules to conclude whether to allow the packet to pass. But in

RADIUS, packet filtering examines rules that an administrator configures, known as "filter profiles," which act as guides to what packets can do what actions on what network. Let's take a closer look.

Let's assume that a certain RADIUS implementation has three filter profiles configured: a "Mailonly" profile, a "FullInet" profile, and a "LocalSurf" profile. These profiles correspond to several account types that a local ISP offers: one for families who simply want email service without the ability to surf the Web, one for those who wish to have a full complement of Internet services, and another for those who enjoy accessing the ISP's local resources: a news server, an about-town page, and perhaps technical support sites.

The profiles feature of RADIUS allows each RADIUS client to store profile information that defines and enforces restrictions on a session. So it is feasible for the ISP to create the Mailonly profile that allows a connection bound to that profile to surf only to the IP of the mail server, only on ports 25 and 110. Similarly, the LocalSurf profile would allow connections only to the IP subnet leased to the ISP.

It's important to note that all RADIUS gear, whether acting as a client or a server, must be configured correctly and consistently for filter profiles to work. Depending on the RADIUS client equipment, if a non-existent or incorrectly configured filter is referenced, the NAS could drop the call, allow no traffic, or allow all traffic. This is obviously not what you, the administrator, desire, as otherwise you wouldn't be configuring a filter!

The RADIUS client looks in the Access-Accept packet to determine whether a filter profile should be applied to the connection.

Framed-AppleTalk-Link

Attribute Number	37
Length	6
Value	INTEGER
Allowed in	Access-Accept
Prohibited in	Access-Request, Access-Reject, Access-Challenge
Presence in Packet	Not required
Maximum Iterations	1

RADIUS supports a session in which the client computer acts as an AppleTalk router. The Framed-AppleTalk-Link attribute identifies that circumstance to the RADIUS client gear on the far side of the connection. If the value of this attribute is greater than zero, then the value is treated as an AppleTalk network number.

The RFC mandates that this attribute *not* be used when the client is not acting as an Apple-Talk router. This attribute is also exclusive of the Framed-AppleTalk-Network attribute: if both are present in the Access-Accept packet, the connection will be unreliable, and the RADIUS client gear is free to disconnect and/or reject the call.

Framed-AppleTalk-Network

Attribute Number	38
Length	6
Value	INTEGER
Allowed in	Access-Accept
Prohibited in	Access-Request, Access-Reject, Access-Challenge
Presence in Packet	Not required
Maximum Iterations	Unlimited

If the dial-up user needs AppleTalk access and is not including the Framed-AppleTalk-Link attribute (thus indicating his desire to act as an AppleTalk router), then the RADIUS client gear will retrieve an AppleTalk network number for the connection from the network that is reflected in the Framed-AppleTalk-Network attribute. If the attribute has a zero value, it is an indication that the client wishes to be assigned an AppleTalk network number by the RADIUS client gear.

The RADIUS RFC permits multiple instances of the Framed-AppleTalk-Network attribute to be included in one Access-Accept packet to allow for redundancy and fail-over should the desired network be unavailable or unwilling to grant access.

Framed-AppleTalk-Zone

Attribute Number	39
Length	3 or more octets
Value	STRING
Allowed in	Access-Accept
Prohibited in	Access-Request, Access-Reject, Access-Challenge
Presence in Packet	Not required
Maximum Iterations	1

This attribute indicates the appropriate AppleTalk zone for the connection. Much like the Class attribute, the value in this attribute is a STRING and is therefore read by the RADIUS client as a string of "undistinguished octets."

Framed-Compression

Attribute Number	13
Length	6
Value	ENUM
Allowed in	Access-Request, Access-Accept
Prohibited in	Access-Reject, Access-Challenge
Presence in Packet	Not required
Maximum Iterations	Unlimited

This attribute states the intent for and type of compression to be used over the connection. The value is of the enumerated type and can range from 0 to 3. Table 3-1 lists the corresponding values and compression types allowed for this attribute.

Table 3-1. Appropriate framed-compression values

Value	Associated compression type
0	None
1	Van-Jacobsen-Header-Compression
2	IPX-Header-Compression
3	Stac-LZS-Compression

For IP-based connections, the Van-Jacobsen compression algorithm is used. For all other connection protocols, the value listed in this attribute determines the compression to be used.

The RADIUS RFC permits multiple instances of the Framed-Compression attribute in the Access-Request and Access-Accept packets; if this is the case, then it is the client gear's responsibility to determine the compression method best suited for that particular connection. It is important to note that if the compression-type value received in a packet is not supported by the RADIUS client gear, it is not under any obligation per the RFCs to honor that request.

Framed-IP-Address

Attribute Number	8
Length	6
Value	IPADDR
Allowed in	Access-Request, Access-Accept
Prohibited in	Access-Reject, Access-Challenge
Presence in Packet	Not required
Maximum Iterations	1

In link-framed connections using such protocols as SLIP and PPP, the Framed-IP-Address attribute carries, quite obviously, the value of the IP address to be assigned to the connection. Depending on the origin of the Access-Request packet, the attribute has the following different meanings:

From the RADIUS client
> The value of this attribute indicates the client's preference in IP address. The RADIUS server does not have to assign this address, although it may do so.

From the server to the client
> The RADIUS server will assign the IP found in this attribute to the connection.

There are exceptions to that rule, however. There are two specific IP values reserved for use by RADIUS. The address 255.255.255.255 is used when the client computer negotiates for the IP it uses—this may be when the user has an assigned static IP address and needs to communicate directly with the IP provisioning equipment in order to get this address. The address 255.255.255.254 is used when the RADIUS client issues the IP address.

Framed-IP-Netmask

Attribute Number	9
Length	6
Value	IPADDR
Allowed in	Access-Request, Access-Accept
Prohibited in	Access-Reject, Access-Challenge
Presence in Packet	Not required
Maximum Iterations	1

This attribute is used when the connection needs a specific netmask number. Even though a client-based DHCP server often assigns netmasks to connections, in certain cases when groups of IP addresses aggregated by CIDR are distributed by the RADIUS server, specific netmasks may be necessary.

While this attribute can appear within an Access-Request packet, the server is not required to honor it, although it may do so.

Framed-IPX-Network

Attribute Number	23
Length	6
Value	INTEGER
Allowed in	Access-Accept
Prohibited in	Access-Request, Access-Reject, Access-Challenge
Presence in Packet	Not required
Maximum Iterations	1

This attribute assigns IPX network numbers. If there is a value in each octet other than 255, then that value represents the IPX network number that should be used. If each octet is 255, then the RADIUS client should choose a number and pass it back to the client.

Framed-MTU

Attribute Number	12
Length	6
Value	INTEGER
Allowed in	Access-Request, Access-Accept
Prohibited in	Access-Reject, Access-Challenge
Presence in Packet	Not required
Maximum Iterations	1

This attribute allows the RADIUS server to set the connection's maximum transfer unit (MTU) size to align communications with the way an administrator has configured his network equipment. Briefly, the MTU setting is the largest packet size that can be transmitted over a connection. If the packet size is larger than this value, then the packet is broken up by routers along the path to the destination and then reassembled at the end point.

The RADIUS server will expect the value of this attribute to be somewhere between 64 and 65,535. Most clients or servers will send this attribute, containing a default MTU size of 1,500, inside an Access-Accept packet.

 It's important to note that only implementations that strictly support RFC 2138 prohibit the Framed-MTU attribute from being passed in Access-Request. The new RADIUS draft supports this, but some implementations may not have been upgraded to support this change.

Framed-Protocol

Attribute Number	7
Length	6
Value	ENUM
Allowed in	Access-Request, Access-Accept
Prohibited in	Access-Reject, Access-Challenge
Presence in Packet	Not required
Maximum Iterations	1

This attribute signals what type of protocol to use over a link-frame connection. The server treats this attribute as a hint if received inside an Access-Request packet and a required condition if received in an Access-Accept packet. The value of this attribute can range from 1 to 6; Table 3-2 lists the values and their corresponding link protocols.

Table 3-2. Framed-protocol attribute values

Value	Link protocol
1	PPP
2	SLIP
3	ARAP
4	Gandalf SLP/MLP
5	Xylogics IPX/SIP
6	X.75 Synchronous

This attribute should be used when the Service-Type attribute is set to Framed.

Framed-Route

Attribute Number	22
Length	3 or more octets
Value	STRING
Allowed in	Access-Accept
Prohibited in	Access-Request, Access-Reject, Access-Challenge
Presence in Packet	Not required
Maximum Iterations	Unlimited

The Framed-Route attribute is used to carry string values corresponding to information to set up a client routing table. The information contained in the STRING-format value is very similar to the information contained in the Windows *netstat* program. Here is a sample output from netstat -rn run on a Windows 2000 Professional machine for reference:

```
===========================================================================
Interface List
0x1 ......................... MS TCP Loopback interface
0x2 ...00 50 56 c0 00 08 ...... VMware Virtual Ethernet Adapter
0x3 ...00 50 56 c0 00 01 ...... VMware Virtual Ethernet Adapter
0x1000005 ...00 a0 cc 60 b6 6d ...... NETGEAR FA310TX Fast Ethernet PCI Adapter
===========================================================================
===========================================================================
Active Routes:
Network Destination        Netmask          Gateway       Interface  Metric
          0.0.0.0          0.0.0.0     192.168.1.10   192.168.1.100  1
        127.0.0.0        255.0.0.0        127.0.0.1       127.0.0.1  1
      192.168.1.0    255.255.255.0    192.168.1.100   192.168.1.100  1
    192.168.1.100  255.255.255.255        127.0.0.1       127.0.0.1  1
    192.168.1.255  255.255.255.255    192.168.1.100   192.168.1.100  1
    192.168.208.0    255.255.255.0    192.168.208.1   192.168.208.1  1
    192.168.208.1  255.255.255.255        127.0.0.1       127.0.0.1  1
  192.168.208.255  255.255.255.255    192.168.208.1   192.168.208.1  1
    192.168.209.0    255.255.255.0    192.168.209.1   192.168.209.1  1
    192.168.209.1  255.255.255.255        127.0.0.1       127.0.0.1  1
  192.168.209.255  255.255.255.255    192.168.209.1   192.168.209.1  1
        224.0.0.0        224.0.0.0    192.168.1.100   192.168.1.100  1
        224.0.0.0        224.0.0.0    192.168.208.1   192.168.208.1  1
        224.0.0.0        224.0.0.0    192.168.209.1   192.168.209.1  1
  255.255.255.255  255.255.255.255    192.168.208.1   192.168.208.1  1
Default Gateway:       192.168.1.10
===========================================================================
Persistent Routes:
  None
Route Table
```

The information in the attribute value must include a destination address, a gateway address, and relevant (but optional) metrics. The RFC suggests that each routing entry be masked in standard CIDR notation. For example, the format for a standard entry would be:

```
<n.n.n.n>/<nn> <n.n.n.n>/<nn> [<metrics>]
```

So an entry directing hosts 192.168.2.0 through 192.168.3.0 to a gateway router at 192.168.10.5 would be:

```
192.168.2.0/23 192.168.10.5/32 1
```

There are several other ways in which this value can be carried and interpreted:

- If some network devices don't support CIDR notation, then the /nn representation can signal the number of bits (8, 16, or 24) to use instead of classful routing. If this is not present, the RADIUS client will resort to the traditional routing of an 8-bit class A address, a 16-bit class B address, or a 24-bit class C address.
- The gateway address can be assigned to the client's interface by passing 0.0.0.0 as the gateway routing entry in this attribute.
- RADIUS implementations are mandated by the RFC to support multiple instances of this attribute inside an Access-Accept packet. Primarily, support for multiple iterations allows custom routing tables to be built for a client, but the applications are not limited to that.

Framed-Routing

Attribute Number	10
Length	6
Value	ENUM
Allowed in	Access-Accept
Prohibited in	Access-Request, Access-Reject, Access-Challenge
Presence in Packet	Not required
Maximum Iterations	1

The routing policies of the client connections are set using the value of this attribute. In some cases, clients may act as routers, passing packets to computers and/or connections other than themselves. In these circumstances, the RADIUS client will need to be able to listen to the broadcasts this client router sends out about its route paths. The values in this attribute, ranging from 0 to 3 and described in Table 3-3, depict the broadcast behaviors for the connection in question.

Table 3-3. Framed-routing attribute values

Value	Broadcast policy
0	None
1	Broadcast routing tables and notifications
2	Listen for routing notification broadcasts
3	Broadcast and listen for notifications

The RFC does not require or recommend a specific routing policy protocol, such as router information protocol (RIP) or open-shortest-path-first (OSPF), nor does it designate specific routing announcements to be broadcast or ignored. In other words, the doors are wide open.

Idle-Timeout

Attribute Number	28
Length	6
Value	ENUM
Allowed in	Access-Accept, Access-Challenge
Prohibited in	Access-Request, Access-Reject
Presence in Packet	Not required
Maximum Iterations	1

An administrator may configure the Idle-Timeout attribute so that the client gear or RADIUS server disconnects a session after a predetermined period of inactivity. The value in this attribute, four-octets long, is the maximum number of seconds a connection may remain active yet idle.

The Idle-Timeout attribute was a good idea for its time. Unfortunately, an administrator must be wary of many small software applications that exist today that are designed to defeat this mechanism. The software ranges in complexity from simple to—wait for it— complex. The lower end of the software simply pings a random server at steady intervals (usually every minute), while the upper end uses sophisticated algorithms to generate traffic more regular yet unpredictable than a ping.

Login-LAT-Group

Attribute Number	36
Length	34
Value	STRING
Allowed in	Access-Request, Access-Accept
Prohibited in	Access-Reject, Access-Challenge
Presence in Packet	Not required
Maximum Iterations	1

The LAT protocol uses a form of authentication based on a bit pattern known as the "group code," and this RADIUS attribute allows the group code to be carried inside Access-Request and Access-Accept packets. Much like other attributes that can be found inside both the Request and Accept packets, its presence inside the Request packet is simply a hint, while its presence in the Accept packet is definite.

If this attribute is present, then the Login-Service attribute must also be present.

Login-LAT-Node

Attribute Number	35
Length	3 or more octets
Value	STRING
Allowed in	Access-Request, Access-Accept
Prohibited in	Access-Reject, Access-Challenge
Presence in Packet	Not required
Maximum Iterations	1

This attribute and its corresponding value indicate the LAT node to which a client should be connected. If this attribute is present in an Access-Accept packet, the Login-Service must also be present.

The Login-LAT-Node attribute operates under the LAT STRING modifications to the RADIUS RFC, and modern implementations should support distinguishing the characters inside the value.

Login-LAT-Port

Attribute Number	63
Length	4 octets
Value	ENUM
Allowed in	Access-Request, Access-Accept
Prohibited in	Access-Reject, Access-Challenge
Presence in Packet	Not required
Maximum Iterations	1

The Login-LAT-Port attribute designates the port to which the client should be connected. Like the other LAT-related attributes, this one must be accompanied by the Login-Service attribute inside an Access-Accept packet to indicate that LAT service is indeed desired.

This attribute also operates under the LAT STRING specification in the RADIUS RFC, meaning some characters inside the string value should be distinguished by the RADIUS implementation.

Login-LAT-Service

Attribute Number	34
Length	3 or more octets
Value	STRING
Allowed in	Access-Request, Access-Accept
Prohibited in	Access-Reject, Access-Challenge
Presence in Packet	Not required
Maximum Iterations	1

There are often other auxiliary services associated with LAT service, and this attribute provides a means for access to those services to be granted to the client. The Login-Service attribute must be included in the same packet and specify the LAT service.

Some LAT services are offered on other machines and may require more information to authenticate, or they may need access to other machines to provision the service. The Login family of standard RADIUS attributes may be used for this purpose in conjunction with the standard LAT attribute family.

This attribute also operates under the LAT STRING specification in the RADIUS RFC, meaning some characters inside the string value should be distinguished by the RADIUS implementation.

Login-IP-Host

Attribute Number	14
Length	6
Value	IPADDR
Allowed in	Access-Request, Access-Accept
Prohibited in	Access-Reject, Access-Challenge
Presence in Packet	Not required
Maximum Iterations	Unlimited

This value carries the IP address of the host that provides the login service for a specific connection. Most commonly this IP address is the address of the actual host, but there are two reserved values that specialize the RADIUS client's behavior. If a value of 255.255.255. 255 (0xFFFFFFFF) is placed in this attribute, then the client needs to assign this host IP itself. If a value of 0.0.0.0 (0x00000000) is placed in this attribute, then the client user should determine and configure this IP address for his connection.

Multiple instances of this packet may be present. The RFC doesn't specify what behavior the RADIUS client should present when it encounters this, but an educated guess would be to allow a selection of host IP addresses for redundancy, fault tolerance, and load balancing.

Login-Service

Attribute Number	15
Length	6
Value	ENUM
Allowed in	Access-Accept
Prohibited in	Access-Request, Access-Reject, Access-Challenge
Presence in Packet	Not required
Maximum Iterations	1

This value specifies the type of service granted to the client. This attribute is intended for use in situations where plain terminal dial-up (i.e., to a shell account) is used. The attribute is exclusive from other framed protocol services. There are eight possible enumerated values for this attribute, which are listed in Table 3-4.

Table 3-4. Login-service attribute values

Value	Login service type
0	Telnet
1	Rlogin
2	TCP Clear
3	PortMaster (Lucent/Livingston)
4	LAT
5	X25-PAD
6	X25-T3POS
7	TCP Clear Quiet

A few of these services deserve further mention.

The standard services that are found most commonly in practice are the Telnet (0) and Rlogin (1) services. Both function to create a connection between the client and the remote host with the RADIUS client acting as a sort of proxy to each party. Most often these services are used to connect users to a Unix shell account or some other terminal service. TCP Clear (2) and TCP Clear Quiet (7) open a direct stream of TCP connectivity between the client and a remote host (the Quiet option simply suppresses announcements from the RADIUS client). The PortMaster (3) service is a proprietary service that connects the user to Livingston (now Lucent) NAS equipment. Finally, the LAT service (4) is used with the Login-LAT family of standard RADIUS attributes.

Login-TCP-Port

Attribute Number	16
Length	6
Value	INTEGER
Allowed in	Access-Accept
Prohibited in	Access-Request, Access-Reject, Access-Challenge
Presence in Packet	Required, unless NAS-IP-Address is present
Maximum Iterations	1

This attribute specifies the remote port used to connect the client to the login service given by the Login-Service attribute. The range of values allowed for this attribute are between 0 and 65,535, though the standard ports below 1,024 are considered privileged and usually require an administrator to configure the service to listen on those ports.

In transactions involving a proxy server, this value can become mangled.

NAS-Identifier

Attribute Number	32
Length	3 or more octets
Value	STRING
Allowed in	Access-Request
Prohibited in	Access-Accept, Access-Reject, Access-Challenge
Presence in Packet	Required, unless NAS-IP-Address is present
Maximum Iterations	1

This attribute identifies the NAS that constructed the Access-Request packet. Most often, the fully qualified domain name (FQDN) is used in the value portion of this attribute (for instance, *local-nas3.raleigh.corp.hasselltech.net*), although the RFC states that the value must be treated as a series of undistinguished octets. The FQDN is often used to eliminate duplicate NAS identifiers and reduce confusion for the client.

This attribute is often vendor specific and each implementation may have customized the use and behavior of this attribute. Additionally, in transactions involving a proxy server, this value can become mangled.

NAS-IP-Address

Attribute Number	4
Length	6
Value	IPADDR
Allowed in	Access-Request
Prohibited in	Access-Accept, Access-Reject, Access-Challenge
Presence in Packet	Required, unless NAS-Identifier is present
Maximum Iterations	1

This attribute specifies the IP address of the NAS gear that requests service on behalf of the client computer. Each implementation may customize the use and behavior of this attribute, but the RADIUS RFC does not permit both this attribute and the NAS-Identifier attribute to be used in the same packet. However, one of the two must be present in any packet.

NAS-Port

Attribute Number	5
Length	6
Value	INTEGER
Allowed in	Access-Request
Prohibited in	Access-Accept, Access-Reject, Access-Challenge
Presence in Packet	Required, unless NAS-Port-Type is present
Maximum Iterations	1

The value in this attribute represents the port to which the client user is connected. It is important to note that this value is *not* the socket port which might identify the protocol the client is using; this value represents the actual, tangible, physical port on the NAS gear to which the client has connected.

The information passed in this value can be useful for identifying load problems or debugging connection problems, either in the NAS itself or possibly in the hunt group connected to that NAS. Most NAS vendors include special software to configure how this information is supplied and most also include special software that will generate algorithms based on the slot number of the NAS, the specific modem, and the NAS port that show call center distribution and other statistical gems.

This attribute *can* co-exist with the NAS-Port-Type attribute. One of the two attributes, though, must always be present in a packet.

NAS-Port-Type

Attribute Number	61
Length	6
Value	ENUM
Allowed in	Access-Request
Prohibited in	Access-Accept, Access-Reject, Access-Challenge
Presence in Packet	Required, unless NAS-Port is present
Maximum Iterations	1

The enumerated value in this attribute depicts what kind of NAS port to which the user has connected. There are 20 physical port types, which are listed in Table 3-5.

Table 3-5. NAS-Port-Type attribute values

Value	Type of port
0	Asynchronous
1	Synchronous
2	ISDN Synchronous
3	ISDN Asynchronous V.120
4	ISDN Asynchronous V.110
5	Virtual
6	PIAFS
7	HDLC Clear Channel
8	X.25
9	X.75
10	G.3 Fax
11	SDSL
12	ADSL-CAP
13	ADSL-DMT
14	IDSL
15	Ethernet
16	XDSL
17	Cable
18	Wireless other
19	Wireless CCITT 802.11

This list of ports covers almost all of the types that would be used in practice. For clarification, I'll discuss a few of the different options that are more commonly found in everyday use:

Asynchronous connections (0)
   The most common type of port used for dial-up clients.

Synchronous (2) connections
   ISDN clients most often use this connection, but they may also use two flavors of asynchronous (3 and 4) connections as well.

PIAFS (6), or PHS Internet Access Forum Standard
   A protocol used primarily in Japan to allow access to devices such as digital cameras, connection concentrators, cellular and mobile telephones, and other handy devices.

Symmetric DSL (11), asymmetric DSL (12 and 13), and DSL over ISDN (14)
   Are offered for DSL types.

802.11b protocol (19)
   Most often used for wireless connections.

Port-Limit

Attribute Number	62
Length	6
Value	INTEGER
Allowed in	Access-Accept, Access-Request
Prohibited in	Access-Reject, Access-Challenge
Presence in Packet	Not required
Maximum Iterations	1

The value of this attribute dictates the upper limit on the number of ports that NAS is authorized to give to the client. In practice, the use of this packet is most often found in support for bonding channels together with ISDN or for multilink point-to-point (MLPPP) protocol, which allows a user to aggregate two modems and phone lines into one IP channel.

There are a couple of caveats to the implementation of the Port-Limit attribute. The problem lies squarely in the fact that the enforcement of this attribute is done at the NAS machine, not at the RADIUS server. In implementations where there is more than one NAS machine, the effective port-limit would be the number of NAS machines present multiplied by the value in Port-Limit. Realistically, some sort of mechanism is needed to keep track of active logins over the entire network lest the efficacy of the Port-Limit attribute be reduced to zero. This exemplifies the need for some sort of third-party session management software, especially in large, distributed networks.

Proxy-State

Attribute Number	33
Length	3 or more octets
Value	STRING
Allowed in	All
Prohibited in	None
Presence in Packet	Not required
Maximum Iterations	Unlimited

This attribute is used when a RADIUS server acts as a proxy and needs to save information about an outstanding request, such as IP addresses, domain names, or other unique integer identifiers. There are a couple of rules to use this attribute, as specified by the RFC:

- If the Proxy-State attribute is found in an Access-Request packet, the information must be included unmodified in the response to the packet, whether the packet is accepted, challenged, or rejected.
- Since multiple instances of this attribute are allowed inside a packet, the order in which they are presented is relevant. When the values of the State attribute are copied, they must be copied in the order in which they were included in the original packet.

It should be noted that some RADIUS client equipment does not follow the RFC specification for the Proxy-State attribute, and this can result in the mangling of any data included in the AVP.

Reply-Message

Attribute Number	18
Length	3 or more octets
Value	STRING
Allowed in	Access-Accept, Access-Reject, Access-Challenge
Prohibited in	Access-Request
Presence in Packet	Not required
Maximum Iterations	Unlimited

This value is used to provide a message to the client in response to another packet. It is often found in Access-Accept messages to provide a welcome message, an error message, or other information to the user.

It is not prudent for an administrator to bet on the end user seeing whatever message is sent in the Reply-Message attribute. Specific consumer/client software may ignore the attribute or present its own notification to the user based on the packet in which this attribute is found.

Service-Type

Attribute Number	6
Length	6
Value	ENUM
Allowed in	Access-Accept, Access-Request
Prohibited in	Access-Reject, Access-Challenge
Presence in Packet	Not required
Maximum Iterations	1

This attribute describes the type of network service that is offered by the RADIUS client gear to the service consumer. The value, a four-octet enumerated integer, works in conjunction with other attributes present in the Access-Request and Access-Accept packets to define and further qualify an offered service. There are 11 specific values appropriate for this attribute, which are listed in Table 3-6.

Table 3-6. Service-Type attribute values

Value	Service type
1	Login
2	Framed
3	Callback Login

Table 3-6. Service-Type attribute values (continued)

Value	Service type
4	Callback Framed
5	Outbound
6	Administrative
7	NAS Prompt
8	Authenticate Only
9	Callback NAS Prompt
10	Call Check
11	Callback Administrative

In the following section, I'll step through each of these predefined service types and discuss their functions within the client transaction.

Login

This value allows the user to have terminal login service. Several standard attributes can be used to further define and enhance the service offered to the user, and these values as well as authentication can be passed using an automated dial-up client rather than sitting at a virtual terminal screen.

Framed

This value indicates that the connection will use a frame protocol such as PPP or SLIP, and each of these protocols will likely require further definition and configuration using additional standard RADIUS attributes. The Framed-* family of attributes defines the IP address, netmask number, MTU, routing, and compression options for a framed connection.

Callback Login

This value indicates the current session will be dropped and the network equipment will call the user back. Apart from that difference, the service is identical to the standard Login (1) service.

Callback Framed

This value directs the RADIUS client to use a frame-based connection upon calling back the client. Apart from that difference, the service is identical to the standard Framed (2) service.

Outbound

Some network service providers may include access to lines available to place outbound calls, and this attribute indicates that the user should be allowed to use those outbound circuits.

Administrative

This value indicates to the RADIUS client that the user should be given administrator rights over its configuration. Some vendors have specific procedures for administrative logins, including entering the administrative user into a special, enhanced, command environment, a root shell on a NAS machine, or simply modifying their privileges so that access to configuration is permitted and then treating the user as a standard client.

NAS Prompt

> This value directs the NAS to prompt the user for a login and password directly to the NAS, which may offer the user a way to execute special commands and configurations normal clients would not have.

Authenticate Only

> Some implementations may store service information and user password and authentication information on different servers. When a client dials in, sometimes all that is needed is a signal of authentication: no services need to be allowed for or provisioned, and this value directs the RADIUS server to simply perform the authentication without any extra overhead. This value would most likely be found in practice in a proxy configuration, in which the authorizing server may not have access to the equipment being provisioned. In this case, the proxy would pass just the authentication information to the authorizing server without any service detail. Upon authenticating, the authorizing server would simply pass the Access-Accept back to the proxy, and the proxy then inserts the relevant service information.

Callback NAS Prompt

> This value indicates that the NAS should call the user back and then prompt him for a login and password to access the NAS machine proper. Apart from that difference, this service is identical to the NAS Prompt (7) service.

Call Check

> In basic terms, the Call Check value allows an administrator to configure his implementation so that authentication takes place before calls are negotiated on the NAS equipment. Let's take a look at this in more detail.

> The typical sequence of events in a RADIUS transaction follows a pattern: the user dials the NAS equipment, the NAS equipment answers and the modem negotiation (the ever-present "screeching") follows, and finally, the server receives the access requests and either accepts or rejects them. The Call Check value allows some slight yet effective modifications to this sequence.

> Say, for instance, a user is in a hotel, which charges for telephone use by the minute. On top of that, the user will incur long-distance charges. It is desirable in these circumstances to allow a call to fail as soon as possible if it is indeed known the call will be rejected. An administrator can configure his RADIUS implementation so that the Access-Request packets are sent before the modem negotiations are finished. If the call will fail, the modems are disconnected, and the user has not had to wait for the negotiation procedures to finish for him to find out his call is rejected. This can save a lot of money on connection charges and, arguably more importantly, it doesn't waste the client's time.

> The implementation of this feature depends a great deal on which vendor manufactures the NAS and RADIUS server, but two keys to check for are the Service-Type attribute being set to Call Check (8), and the User-Name attribute being the distinguished name or the called station identifier.

Callback Administrative

> This value indicates that the NAS should drop the immediate connection and call the user back with the connection set up so that the called-back user has administrative privileges of the NAS machine itself. Apart from that difference, this service is identical to the Administrative (6) service.

Session-Timeout

Attribute Number	27
Length	6
Value	INTEGER
Allowed in	Access-Accept, Access-Challenge
Prohibited in	Access-Request, Access-Reject
Presence in Packet	Not required
Maximum Iterations	1

This attribute indicates the maximum length of time in seconds that a user may remain connected to the network before the RADIUS client will kick him off. This is primarily used to enforce connect-time limits on certain account package types or to prevent camping on a line. (*Camping* is when a user treats a non-dedicated connection, such as a dial-up account, as a dedicated connection by keeping the line up 24 hours a day, 7 days a week.)

Much like the Idle-Timeout attribute, there are many software packages meant for the client side that detect a disconnected session and immediately reconnect it. There is no inherent mechanism on the RADIUS server, at least as specified in the RFC, to prevent usage of this software, since the Session-Timeout value is just a counter that is stateless and memory-less. It can be and is reset each time a new connection is made.

State

Attribute Number	24
Length	3 or more octets
Value	STRING
Allowed in	Access-Accept, Access-Request, Access-Challenge
Prohibited in	Access-Reject
Presence in Packet	Not required
Maximum Iterations	1

The State attribute, valid over an entire connection session, is an implementation-specific attribute that can be used for a variety of purposes. For example, in a proxy implementation, some session information may need to be saved and accessed to expedite authentication or provide services for inherently stateless connections.

The State attribute is part of a group of interchangeable yet singly required attributes: at all times one of the User-Password, CHAP-Password, or State attributes must be present in a packet. How the RADIUS client behaves when it sees a State attribute depends on the type of packet in which the attribute is found.

- If the State attribute is found in an Access-Accept packet, then the RADIUS client must include the value of the attribute in any new Access-Request packets. For this to work properly, the value of the Terminate-Action attribute must also be set to RADIUS-Request. (See the next attribute for more information on Terminate-Action.)

- If the State attribute is found in an Access-Challenge packet, then the value of the State attribute must be included, unmodified, in the Access-Request packet sent in response to the challenge. It is NOT permitted for the RADIUS client to interpret the value of State, and no operation of the core protocol may be affected by the value of State.

Terminate-Action

Attribute Number	29
Length	6
Value	ENUM
Allowed in	Access-Accept
Prohibited in	Access-Request, Access-Reject, Access-Challenge
Presence in Packet	Not required
Maximum Iterations	1

This attribute passes a value that dictates the behavior that the RADIUS client gear should portray upon terminating a client's connection. There are two possible values for this attribute, neither of which are required to be supported by the RADIUS server (but the lack of support of these values cannot affect the standard operation of the core RADIUS protocol): a 0, to indicate the server should perform its default termination action; and a 1, to indicate the client desires to have the RADIUS client send new Access-Request packets upon a session's completion.

User-Name

Attribute Number	1
Length	3 or more octets
Value	STRING
Allowed in	Access-Request, Access-Accept
Prohibited in	Access-Reject, Access-Challenge
Presence in Packet	Not required
Maximum Iterations	1

This attribute carries the distinguished name of the client requesting access to services on the network. Since usernames come in all sizes and flavors, there is not a specified maximum length for this value. It has been recommended by the RADIUS committee and those who follow its proceedings that support for a larger username space be provided (up to 64 bytes in length) to allow the implementation-specific RADIUS client gear to perform its own compliancy and validity checking. This allows each administrator to customize the requirements for a valid username without having a standard dictate to them how usernames are constructed.

There are no specific requirements for the format in which these usernames must be represented, but there are a number of possible ways in which usernames are commonly passed in the User-Name attribute. Monolithic, or alphanumeric, usernames consist of all letters and numbers. UTF-8 characters are also supported. Additionally, usernames can be passed that conform to the Network Access Identifier (NAI) ASN.1 format—this is often known as the "distinguished name"—or some other format common to both the client and the RADIUS implementation. Because of this flexibility, administrators have a wide realm of possibilities for creating username standards.

RADIUS servers may also use a username to determine appropriate behavior for a transaction. For instance, if a username is passed in realm format (i.e., *WEST/aslyter*), then the RADIUS server may change its configuration to act as a proxy for that transaction, forwarding the request to an appropriate server within the WEST realm. Of course, the username can be ignored and simply passed, in which the RADIUS server acts like a transparent proxy and simply hands the requests on without filtering or preprocessing.

User-Password

Attribute Number	2
Length	18 to 130 octets
Value	STRING
Allowed in	Access-Request
Prohibited in	Access-Accept, Access-Reject, Access-Challenge
Presence in Packet	Required, unless CHAP-Password is present
Maximum Iterations	1

This attribute is designed to carry authentication information that a user provides in order to gain access to network services. Primarily, the content of this value will be an encrypted password, but sometimes it can be the response from an Access-Challenge packet sent to the client from the RADIUS server. Most commonly, the length of the value is 16 octets, which is the RFC minimum, but the RFC also permits the value of this attribute to span as long as 130 octets.

As mentioned in Chapters 1 and 2, the presence of the User-Password attribute typically indicates that the given transaction will use PAP authentication in lieu of CHAP. Refer to Chapter 2 for an explanation of the hiding and encrypting process used in PAP authentication.

Vendor-Specific

Attribute Number	26
Length	7 or more octets
Value	STRING
Allowed in	Access-Accept, Access-Request, Access-Challenge
Prohibited in	Access-Reject
Presence in Packet	Not required
Maximum Iterations	Unlimited

This attribute is used to carry attributes that are not specified in the RADIUS RFC. Vendors, NAS manufacturers, and others may want to transmit various implementation-specific information to the client and server and, thus, need a way to pass that information. However, this vendor information passed in addition to the standard global attributes absolutely cannot affect the operation of the base RADIUS protocol in any way. In Chapter 2, I discussed the format of a vendor-specific AVP and how one is carried inside this attribute.

Of particular interest is the type of this attribute. It is listed as a STRING type, but effectively it is seen as a pattern of undistinguished octets—this is to ensure the parts of the implementation that are not aware of the vendor-specific values do not misconfigure themselves or otherwise do detriment to the connection. Further, the value of the VSA within the vendor-specific AVP actually has several specification fields—think of them as "microfields" that further qualify the VSA. This eliminates any confusion and conflict between attributes specific to a vendor's implementation and attributes generally available per the RADIUS RFC.

## CHAPTER 4

RADIUS Accounting

ISPs often manage points of presence over several locations, most likely geographically dispersed. All of these points of presence require protection to guard against unauthorized use of the expensive network to which they allow access. Although the front line of defense may (and should) be a robust and extensible form of authentication (to verify a user's declared identity) and authorization (to provide a user with only the services to which he is entitled), much valuable information can be gleaned from data collected about users' activities on the network. Which user logged on? When did she do so? What services was he granted?

The data becomes even more useful when it is compiled to analyze a group of users. What is the average call time for a user? How much data does that user transfer? Do I, as a system administrator, need to set a time limit for a single session so as to protect limited dial-in resources? Do I have users that are abusing an on-demand connection? All of these questions can be answered using information mined from the accounting process.

RADIUS supports a full-featured accounting protocol subset, which allows it to satisfy all requirements of the AAA model. This chapter describes the design, operation, packets, and attributes that are specific and germane to RADIUS accounting.

Key Points in RADIUS Accounting

The design of accounting in RADIUS is based upon three major characteristics:

Accounting will be based on a client/server model.
> The RADIUS accounting machine is the server to the RADIUS client gear, which acts as the client. The client passes the usage data to the RADIUS server for processing. The RADIUS server acknowledges successful receipt of the data. It is also possible for the RADIUS server to act as an accounting proxy, much like the similar capability in the authentication and authorization realms.

Communications between devices will be secure.

All data is passed to and from the RADIUS server and the client gear through the use of a shared secret, which is never transmitted across the wire.

RADIUS accounting will be extensible.

The format of the accounting attributes is much like those of the authentication and authorization attributes, in that most of the services offered by the implementations can be defined and qualified using AVPs. AVPs can be added and modified to an existing implementation without disrupting the functionality already in use.

Basic Operation

All communications regarding RADIUS accounting are done with an Accounting-Request packet. A client that is participating in the RADIUS accounting process will generate an Accounting Start packet, which is a specific kind of Accounting-Request packet. This packet includes information on which service has been provisioned and on the user for which these services are provided. This packet is sent to the RADIUS accounting server, which will then acknowledge receipt of the data. When the client is finished with the network services, it will send to the accounting server an Accounting Stop packet (again, a specialized Accounting-Request packet), which will include the service delivered; usage statistics such as time elapsed, amount transferred, average speed; and other details. The accounting server acknowledges receipt of the stop packet, and all is well. If the server does not or cannot handle the contents of the Accounting-Request packet, it is not allowed to send a receipt acknowledgment to the client.

In this instance, the RFC recommends that a client continue to send its packets to the accounting server when it has not received an acknowledgment that its Accounting-Request packet has been processed. In fact, in large distributed networks, it is desirable to have several accounting servers act in a round-robin fashion to handle failover and redundancy needs. An administrator can carry this mentality further and designate certain accounting servers to handle different requests—one for his dial-up users, one for his DSL customers, and yet another for ISDN connections. Additionally, the proxy functionality present in the authentication and authorization realms of RADIUS are also allowed in the accounting phase, as the accounting server may make requests of other servers to assist in the processing of Accounting-Request packets.

More on Proxying

RADIUS accounting proxies act in much the same way as RADIUS authentication/authorization proxies do. Consider the following process:

1. The RADIUS client gear sends the Accounting Start packet to the accounting server.

2. The receiving accounting server logs the packet. It may then add the Proxy-State attribute and accompanying details (though it is not required to do so). It updates the request authenticator and then forwards the information to a remote machine.

3. This remote machine logs the incoming, forwarded packet. It then does what the first server could not do (that is to say, it performs the action that was required of the proxy), retains and copies all of the Proxy-State attributes *exactly as they appeared*, and sends an Accounting-Response packet back to the original forwarding server.

4. The original forwarding server receives the acknowledgment, strips out the Proxy-State information, constructs and adds the Response Authenticator, and sends the modified acknowledgment response back to the RADIUS client gear.

Figure 4-1 shows the flow of this process.

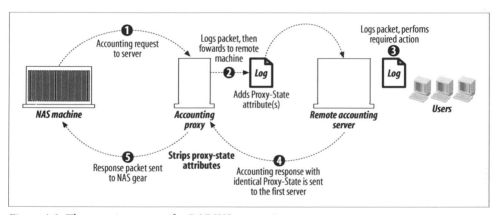

Figure 4-1. The proxying process for RADIUS accounting

The Accounting Packet Format

As mentioned in Chapter 2, the RADIUS protocol uses a UDP foundation to transmit packets between clients, servers, and proxies. While the original RADIUS accounting RFC (number 2139, to be exact) specified that accounting transactions should take place on port 1646, the latest RFC (2866) changed the port to 1813, because port 1646 was already assigned to the sa-msg-port service.

The packets are broken down into four distinct regions, which are discussed next.

Code

The code region is one-octet long and indicates the type of RADIUS accounting information transmitted in that packet. Packets with invalid code fields are thrown away without notification. Valid codes are:

4

    Accounting-Request

5

    Accounting-Response

Identifier

The identifier region is one-octet long and is used to perform threading, or the automated linking of initial requests and subsequent replies. RADIUS accounting servers can generally intercept duplicate messages by examining such factors as the source IP address, the source UDP port, the time span between the suspect messages, and the identifier field.

Length

The length region is two-octets long and is used to specify the length of a RADIUS accounting message. The value in this field is calculated by analyzing the code, identifier, length, authenticator, and attribute fields and finding their sum. The length field is checked to ensure data integrity when an accounting server receives a packet. Valid length values range between 20 and 4095.

The RFC specification requires certain behaviors of RADIUS servers with regard to incorrect length data. If the accounting server receives a transmission with a message longer than the length field, it ignores all data past the end point designated in the length field. Conversely, if the server receives a shorter message than the length field reports, the server will discard the message.

Authenticator

The authenticator region, often 16-octets long, is the field in which the integrity of the packet's payload is inspected and verified. In this field, the most important octet—the value used to authenticate replies from the accounting server—is transmitted before any other.

There are two distinct types of authenticators: the request and response authenticators. Request authenticators, consisting of 16-octet MD5 checksums, are computed using a hash generated from the code, identifier, length, attributes, shared secrets, and 16 "zeroed-out" octets. The value returned from this hash is then placed into the authenticator field.

It's important to notice the distinction between how the request authenticator is computed in the accounting phase and the authentication/authorization phase. The difference lies squarely in the fact that in accounting packets, the User-Password attribute is not included.

The response authenticator is calculated in much the same way as the request authenticator. An MD5 hash is generated using the values from the code, identifier, length, request authenticator from the original request, and response attributes; the value from this hash is placed in the authenticator field.

It also is important to point out that some early RADIUS and NAS implementations send some accounting packets with the authenticator region set to all zeroes. While the RFCs have been modified to specifically forbid this behavior, for backward compatibility purposes some RADIUS servers can accept packets exhibiting this behavior.

Reliability of Accounting

While the specification for RADIUS accounting is promising, experience sees that accounting packets are not a sure, 100% certainty. For example, if a client sends accounting packets to a server but receives no acknowledgment or response, he will continue to send the same packet for only a limited time. This results in some sessions with inconsistent records. This presents problems with operations that require great consistency and accuracy: billing is a prime but certainly not sole example. While progress is being made in improving the reliability of the accounting mechanism (mainly with interim records, which are covered in Chapter 9), you should be aware of the problem.

Accounting Packet Types

At this point, we have covered the structure of the packets that RADIUS uses to transmit accounting data. But we need to establish the identity and properties of these specific packets. There are two RADIUS packet types that are relevant to the accounting phase of an AAA transaction:

- Accounting-Request
- Accounting-Response

The next section will step through these packets and detail their intent, format, and structure.

Accounting-Request

Packet Type	Request
Code	4
Identifier	Unique for each request; unique for each transmission of modified data
Authenticator	Request
Attribute Data	0 or more attributes

Accounting-Request packets are sent from the client to the server. Remember that a client can be a true RADIUS client or another RADIUS server acting as a proxy. The client sends the packet with the code field set to 4. When the server receives this request packet, it is required to transmit an acknowledgment to the client unless it cannot handle or process the packet. In this case, it cannot transmit anything to the client.

With the exceptions of the User-Password, CHAP-Password, Reply-Message, and State attributes, any other attribute allowed in an Access-Request or Access-Accept packet can be used inside an Accounting-Request packet.

 Chapter 3 discusses all standard RADIUS attributes and their properties, including the packets in which they are allowed to be included. Check there for a complete overview of packet presence requirements.

There are a couple more caveats to presence in the packet. As mentioned in Chapter 2, the NAS-IP-Address and NAS-Identifier attributes are mutually exclusive, meaning that one or the other must be included in a packet, but not both. The RFC recommends distinguishing the NAS port or type of port in the packet by using the NAS-Port or NAS-Port-Type attributes unless that information is superfluous to the service. Additionally, the Framed-IP-Address must include the real IP address of the user.

Accounting-Response

Packet Type	Response
Code	5
Identifier	Identical to corresponding Accounting-Request
Authenticator	Response
Attribute Data	0 or more attributes

The Accounting-Response packets are primarily designed as acknowledgment packets to be sent from the accounting server to the client, indicating that the request from the client has been received and logged. If the packet was indeed processed and logged successfully, the RFC mandates that the code field of the acknowledgment section be set to 5 to indicate a response. Since the identifier of the response packet is identical to the corresponding Accounting-Request field, the client can easily match the two packets together to keep track of which requests have been fulfilled and which are outstanding.

Not only do Accounting-Response packets not have to contain any attributes, but in practice it is rare for them to do so. However, in the case of a proxy transaction, the Proxy-State attribute can be included in the packet. As well, any vendor-specific attributes may be included in Accounting-Response packets.

Accounting-specific Attributes

In the following section, I'll cover the attributes of the global RADIUS space that are specific to the accounting phase of an AAA transaction. Much like in Chapter 3, each of the current 12 accounting-specific attributes will be a separate tidbit of information, including an at-a-glance properties chart and a short discussion of key points and important considerations. Again, the Appendix is a chart of the entire global RADIUS attribute list, covering all phases of the AAA model, and should serve as a useful quick reference.

Acct-Status-Type

Attribute Number	40
Length	6
Value	ENUM
Allowed in	Accounting-Request
Prohibited in	Accounting-Response
Presence in Packet	Required
Maximum Iterations	1

This attribute indicates whether the Accounting-Request packet is being sent upon the user first authenticating and connecting to the network or upon the user finishing use of the services and disconnecting. It can also be used to mark when to start and stop accounting should the RADIUS client gear require rebooting or other system maintenance. Note that when RADIUS client gear crashes, stop records in general are not sent to the accounting server. Obviously, this has the potential to mess up accounting data, and a crashed client is not all that uncommon.

The payload value of the attribute contains 15 possible values, each of which are listed in Table 4-1.

Table 4-1. Values for the Acct-Status-Type attribute

Value	Status type
1	Start
2	Stop
3	Interim-Update
7	Accounting-On

Table 4-1. Values for the Acct-Status-Type attribute (continued)

Value	Status type
8	Accounting-Off
9–14	Reserved; used for tunnel accounting
15	Reserved; used for failed attempts

Acct-Delay-Time

Attribute Number	41
Length	6
Value	INTEGER
Allowed in	Accounting-Request
Prohibited in	Accounting-Response
Presence in Packet	Not required
Maximum Iterations	1

The Acct-Delay-Time attribute records how many seconds the client has been trying to push this packet through to the accounting server. While the significance of this attribute may seem less than overwhelming on the outset, by subtracting this value from the time a packet arrives at the accounting server, the time of the request-generating event (a sign-on, sign-off, termination, etc.) can be computed. Network transit time is not factored into this calculation.

As I mentioned earlier, when the attributes of any accounting packet change, the identifier associated with the packet must be changed as well. This rule carries over into this attribute specifically: when the delay time is changed, a new identifier must be generated for the new packet.

Acct-Input-Octets

Attribute Number	42
Length	6
Value	INTEGER
Allowed in	Accounting-Request, interim updates
Prohibited in	Accounting-Response
Presence in Packet	Not required
Maximum Iterations	1

This attribute, which can only be found in Accounting-Request packets with Acct-Status-Type set to code 2 (Stop) or interim updates (covered in Chapter 9), indicates the number of incoming octets passed through a specific client port during one session.

Acct-Output-Octets

Attribute Number	43
Length	6
Value	INTEGER
Allowed in	Accounting-Request
Prohibited in	Accounting-Response
Presence in Packet	Not required
Maximum Iterations	1

The opposite of `Acct-Input-Octets`, this attribute, which can only be found in `Accounting-Request` packets with the `Acct-Status-Type` set to code 2 (Stop), indicates the number of outgoing octets transmitted through a specific client port during one session.

Acct-Session-ID

Attribute Number	44
Length	3 or more octets
Value	STRING
Allowed in	Accounting-Request
Prohibited in	Accounting-Response
Presence in Packet	Required
Maximum Iterations	1

This attribute is used to uniquely identify a session so that accounting stop and start records can be collated and recorded accurately. There are a few considerations as to the packets that these attributes can be found in:

Accounting-Request packets
> are required to have `Acct-Session-ID`.

Access-Request packets
> are allowed to contain this attribute. If this is the case, then the RADIUS client gear is required to use the same session ID in all packets pertaining to that connection for the duration of that session.

The RFC requires that this session ID be printed using the UTF-8 10646 character set. From RFC 2866: "For example, one implementation uses a string with an 8-digit upper case hexadecimal number, [sic] the first two digits increment on each reboot (wrapping every 256 reboots) and the next 6 digits counting from 0 for the first person logging in after a reboot up to 2^{24-1}, about 16 million. Other encodings are possible."

In practice, however, RADIUS client equipment tends to not send the `Acct-Session-ID` attributes using unique values. Many reuse these values across reboots, which can make tracking a session in its entirety using accounting data much more difficult.

Acct-Authentic

Attribute Number	45
Length	6
Value	ENUM
Allowed in	Accounting-Request
Prohibited in	Accounting-Response
Presence in Packet	Not required
Maximum Iterations	1

This optional attribute indicates the method with which the user's declared identity was verified. There are three possible values for this attribute, which are listed in Table 4-2.

Table 4-2. Values for the Acct-Authentic attribute

Value	Authentication method
1	RADIUS
2	Local
3	Remote

The second value, "Local," within the context of this attribute signifies that the client verified the identity of this user of its own accord through an authentication method other than RADIUS. This can cause problems when matching accounting data to authentication/authorization information, since no authorization data exists for the session.

Acct-Session-Time

Attribute Number	46
Length	6
Value	INTEGER
Allowed in	Accounting-Request, interim updates
Prohibited in	Accounting-Response
Presence in Packet	Not required
Maximum Iterations	1

This attribute, found in Accounting-Request packets and interim records, indicates the time in seconds that a user has been connected. Note that this attribute can only be present when the Acct-Status-Type attribute inside the request packet is set to code 2 (Stop).

Acct-Input-Packets

Attribute Number	47
Length	6
Value	INTEGER

Allowed in	Accounting-Request, interim updates
Prohibited in	Accounting-Response
Presence in Packet	Not required
Maximum Iterations	1

This attribute, which can only be found in Accounting-Request packets with the Acct-Status-Type set to code 2 (Stop) and in interim accounting updates, indicates the number of incoming packets passed through a specific RADIUS client port to a framed user during one session.

Acct-Output-Packets

Attribute Number	48
Length	6
Value	INTEGER
Allowed in	Accounting-Request, interim updates
Prohibited in	Accounting-Response
Presence in Packet	Not required
Maximum Iterations	1

The opposite of Acct-Input-Packets, this attribute, which can only be found in Accounting-Request packets with the Acct-Status-Type set to code 2 (Stop) and in interim accounting updates, indicates the number of outgoing packets transmitted through a specific client port from a framed user during one session.

Acct-Terminate-Cause

Attribute Number	49
Length	6
Value	ENUM
Allowed in	Accounting-Request
Prohibited in	Accounting-Response
Presence in Packet	Not required
Maximum Iterations	1

The Acct-Terminate-Cause attribute indicates the reason, if possible and applicable, that a user's session was ended. Like a good number of the other accounting attributes, the request packet must contain the Acct-Status-Type attribute set to Stop (code 2).

Listed in Table 4-3 are the 18 possible values for this attribute.

Table 4-3. Values for the Acct-Terminate-Cause attribute

Value	Termination cause
1	User Request
2	Lost Carrier

Table 4-3. Values for the Acct-Terminate-Cause attribute (continued)

Value	Termination cause
3	Lost Service
4	Idle Timeout
5	Session Timeout
6	Admin Reset
7	Admin Reboot
8	Port Error
9	NAS Error
10	NAS Request
11	NAS Reboot
12	Port Unneeded
13	Port Preempted
14	Port Suspended
15	Service Unavailable
16	Callback
17	User Error
18	Host Request

Let's take a closer look at each of these termination causes:

User Request
> The user initiated the termination by logging off.

Lost Carrier
> The port could no longer hold DCD.

Lost Service
> For some reason, the service is unavailable for continued provision. Connection inter-
> ruptions are the most likely cause.

Idle Timeout
> The configured limit for an idle connection was reached.

Session Timeout
> The configured limit for the length of a single session was reached.

Admin Reset
> The system administrator reset hardware necessary to continue the connection.

Admin Reboot
> The system administrator is terminating all service on a particular machine, most likely
> immediately preceding a reboot.

Port Error
> The NAS gear encountered an error in the port; service could not be continued.

NAS Error

The NAS gear encountered an error somewhere other than in the port; service could not be continued.

NAS Request

The NAS gear terminated the connection for another, unknown reason.

NAS Reboot

The NAS gear "crashed" and required a reboot. (This attribute is used almost exclusively for nonadministrative restarts.) Unfortunately, this is not a reliable mechanism, as this signal is often not sent on a reboot. Lobby your NAS manufacturer for a fix if your equipment is affected by this.

Port Unneeded

The NAS, through some algorithm, determined that the port was no longer needed to continue maintaining a certain threshold of quality of service.

Port Preempted

A higher priority thread required the use of the port.

Port Suspended

The NAS requested to end a virtual session by suspending it.

Service Unavailable

For whatever reason, the NAS gear is unavailable to service the request.

Callback

The NAS is ending the current connection so that it may dial the user back to continue his service.

User Error

The user input data incorrectly.

Host Request

The host ended the session predictably and as expected.

Acct-Multi-Session-ID

Attribute Number	50
Length	3 or more octets
Value	STRING
Allowed in	Accounting-Request
Prohibited in	Accounting-Response
Presence in Packet	Not required
Maximum Iterations	Unlimited

This attribute contains a unique ID that can be used to "thread" data from multiple related sections together into one log file. The Acct-Session-ID for each session would be unique, but all would be linked by a common Acct-Multi-Session-ID. This is useful for applications where multilinking and channel-bonding services, such as multilink PPP, are provided and supported. More details on these services are provided in Chapter 6.

Acct-Link-Count

Attribute Number	51
Length	6
Value	INTEGER
Allowed in	Accounting-Request
Prohibited in	Accounting-Response
Presence in Packet	Not required
Maximum Iterations	Unlimited

This attribute indicates the number of current sessions in a multilink transaction. The way this value is determined is of particular interest. Let's examine it more closely.

The value field simply shows the number of times links have been observed by the accounting server whose connections are using the same Acct-Multi-Session-ID. The following is a tabulation example of link counts. By using these link counts *and* enumerating each Accounting Stop packet received, the accounting server can determine when its recordkeeping is complete for any given multilink session:

Multi-Session-ID	Session-ID	Status-Type	Link-Count
52	21	Start	1
52	22	Start	2
52	23	Start	3
52	22	Stop	3
52	21	Stop	3
52	24	Start	4
52	23	Stop	4
52	22	Stop	4

## CHAPTER 5

Getting Started with FreeRADIUS

Up to this point, I've talked about the theoretical underpinnings of both the authentication-authorization-accounting (AAA) architecture as well as the specific implementation of AAA characteristics that is the RADIUS protocol. I will now focus on practical applications of RADIUS: implementing it, customizing it for your specific needs, and extending its capabilities to meet other needs in your business. First, though, I need a product that talks RADIUS.

Enter FreeRADIUS.

Introduction to FreeRADIUS

The developers of FreeRADIUS speak on their product and its development, from the FreeRADIUS web site:

> FreeRADIUS is one of the most modular and featureful [sic] RADIUS servers available today. It has been written by a team of developers who have more than a decade of collective experience in implementing and deploying RADIUS software, in software engineering, and in Unix package management. The product is the result of synergy between many of the best-known names in free software-based RADIUS implementations, including several developers of the Debian GNU/Linux operating system, and is distributed under the GNU GPL (version 2).

FreeRADIUS is a complete rewrite, ground-up compilation of a RADIUS server. The configuration files exhibit many similarities to the old Livingston RADIUS server. The product includes support for:

- Limiting the maximum number of simultaneous logons, even on a per-user basis
- More than one DEFAULT entry, with each being capable of "falling through" to the next
- Permitting and denying access to users based on the *huntgroup* to which they are connected
- Setting certain parameters to be huntgroup specific

- Intelligent "hints" files that select authentication protocols based on the syntax of the username
- Executing external programs upon successful login
- Using the $INCLUDE filename format with configuration, users, and dictionary files
- Vendor-specific attributes
- Acting as a proxy RADIUS server

FreeRADIUS supports the following popular NAS equipment:

- 3Com/USR Hiper Arc Total Control
- 3Com/USR NetServer
- 3Com/USR TotalControl
- Ascend Max 4000 family
- Cisco Access Server family
- Cistron PortSlave
- Computone PowerRack
- Cyclades PathRAS
- Livingston PortMaster
- Multitech CommPlete Server
- Patton 2800 family

FreeRADIUS is available for a wide range of platforms, including Linux, FreeBSD, OpenBSD, OSF/Unix, and Solaris. For the purposes of this book, I will focus on FreeRADIUS running under Linux. Also, as of this printing, a stable Version 1.0 of the product had not been released. However, development of the server is very stable, careful, and somewhat slow, so changes to the procedures mentioned are unlikely. In the event a procedure does change, it's likely to be a relatively small modification. Always check the FreeRADIUS web site for up-to-date details.

Installing FreeRADIUS

At present, the FreeRADIUS team doesn't offer precompiled binaries. The best way to start off is to grab the latest source code, compressed using tar and *gzip*, from the FreeRADIUS web site at *http://www.freeradius.org*. Once the file is on your computer, execute the following command to uncompress the file:

```
tar -zxvf freeradius.tar.gz
```

Next, you'll need to compile FreeRADIUS. Make sure your system at least has *gcc*, *glibc*, *binutils*, and *gmake* installed before trying to compile. To begin compiling, change to the directory where your uncompressed source code lies and execute *./configure* from the command line. You can also run *./configure -flags* and customize the settings for the flags in Table 5-1.

Table 5-1. Optional configuration flags for FreeRADIUS

Flag	Purpose	Default
--enable-shared[=PKGS]	Builds shared libraries.	Yes
--enable-static[=PKGS]	Builds static libraries.	Yes
--enable-fast-install[=PKGS]	Optimizes the resulting files for fastest installation.	Yes
--with-gnu-ld	Makes the procedure assume the C compiler uses *GNU ID*.	No
--disable-libtool-lock	Avoids locking problems. This may break parallel builds.	Not applicable
--with-logdir=DIR	Specifies the directory for log files.	LOCALSTATEDIR/log
--with-radacctdir=DIR	Specifies the directory for detail files.	LOGDIR/radacct
--with-raddbdir=DIR	Specifies the directory for configuration files.	SYSCONFDIR/raddb
--with-dict-nocase	Makes the dictionary case insensitive.	Yes
--with-ascend-binary	Includes support for attributes provided with the Ascend binary filter.	Yes
--with-threads	Uses threads if they're supported and available.	Yes
--with-snmp	Compiles SNMP support into the binaries.	Yes
--with-mysql-include-dir=DIR	Specifies where the include files for MySQL can be found.	Not applicable
--with-mysql-lib-dur=DIR	Specifies where the dictionary files for MySQL can be found.	Not applicable
--with-mysql-dir-DIR	Specifies where MySQL is installed on the local system.	Not applicable
--disable-ltdl-install	Does not install *libltdl*.	Not applicable
--with-static-modules=QUOTED-MODULE-LIST	Compiles the list of modules statically.	Not applicable
--enable-developer	Turns on extra developer warnings in the compiler.	Not applicable

Commonly, the following locations are used when installing a RADIUS product (these practices go back to the Cistron RADIUS server):

Binaries
    /usr/local/bin and */usr/local/sbin*

Manual (man) pages
   /usr/local/man

Configuration files
   /etc/raddb

Log files
   /var/log and */var/log/radacct*

To make the compiler use these locations automatically, execute:

```
./configure --localstatedir=/var --sysconfdir=/etc
```

The programs will then be configured to compile. The rest of this chapter will assume that you installed FreeRADIUS in these locations.

Next, type make. This will compile the binaries. Finally, type make install. This will place all of the files in the appropriate locations. It will also install configuration files if this server has not had a RADIUS server installed before. Otherwise, the procedure will not overwrite your existing configuration and will report to you on what files it did not install.

At this point, your base FreeRADIUS software is installed. Before you begin, though, you'll need to customize some of the configuration files so that they point to machines and networks specific to your configuration. Most of these files are located in */etc/raddb*. The following files are contained by default:

```
radius:/etc/raddb # ls -al
total 396
drwxr-xr-x   2 root     root         4096 Apr 10 10:39 .
drwxr-xr-x   3 root     root         4096 Apr 10 10:18 ..
-rw-r--r--   1 root     root          635 Apr 10 10:18 acct_users
-rw-r--r--   1 root     root         3431 Apr 10 10:18 attrs
-rw-r--r--   1 root     root          595 Apr 10 11:02 clients
-rw-r--r--   1 root     root         2235 Apr 10 10:39 clients.conf
-rw-r--r--   1 root     root        12041 Apr 10 10:18 dictionary
-rw-r--r--   1 root     root        10046 Apr 10 10:39 dictionary.acc
-rw-r--r--   1 root     root         1320 Apr 10 10:39 dictionary.aptis
-rw-r--r--   1 root     root        54018 Apr 10 10:39 dictionary.ascend
-rw-r--r--   1 root     root        11051 Apr 10 10:39 dictionary.bay
-rw-r--r--   1 root     root         4763 Apr 10 10:39 dictionary.cisco
-rw-r--r--   1 root     root         1575 Apr 10 10:39 dictionary.compat
-rw-r--r--   1 root     root         1576 Apr 10 10:39 dictionary.erx
-rw-r--r--   1 root     root          375 Apr 10 10:39 dictionary.foundry
-rw-r--r--   1 root     root          279 Apr 10 10:39 dictionary.freeradius
-rw-r--r--   1 root     root         2326 Apr 10 10:39 dictionary.livingston
-rw-r--r--   1 root     root         2396 Apr 10 10:39 dictionary.microsoft
-rw-r--r--   1 root     root          190 Apr 10 10:39 dictionary.nomadix
-rw-r--r--   1 root     root         1537 Apr 10 10:39 dictionary.quintum
-rw-r--r--   1 root     root         8563 Apr 10 10:39 dictionary.redback
-rw-r--r--   1 root     root          457 Apr 10 10:39 dictionary.shasta
-rw-r--r--   1 root     root         2958 Apr 10 10:39 dictionary.shiva
-rw-r--r--   1 root     root         1274 Apr 10 10:39 dictionary.tunnel
-rw-r--r--   1 root     root        63265 Apr 10 10:39 dictionary.usr
```

```
-rw-r--r--    1 root     root       2199 Apr 10 10:39  dictionary.versanet
-rw-r--r--    1 root     root       1767 Apr 10 10:18  hints
-rw-r--r--    1 root     root       1603 Apr 10 10:18  huntgroups
-rw-r--r--    1 root     root       2289 Apr 10 10:39  ldap.attrmap
-rw-r--r--    1 root     root        830 Apr 10 10:18  naslist
-rw-r--r--    1 root     root        856 Apr 10 10:18  naspasswd
-rw-r--r--    1 root     root       9533 Apr 10 10:39  postgresql.conf
-rw-r--r--    1 root     root       4607 Apr 10 10:39  proxy.conf
-rw-r--r--    1 root     root      27266 Apr 10 10:57  radiusd.conf
-rw-r--r--    1 root     root      27232 Apr 10 10:39  radiusd.conf.in
-rw-r--r--    1 root     root       1175 Apr 10 10:18  realms
-rw-r--r--    1 root     root       1405 Apr 10 10:39  snmp.conf
-rw-r--r--    1 root     root       9089 Apr 10 10:39  sql.conf
-rw-r--r--    1 root     root       6941 Apr 10 10:18  users
-rw-r--r--    1 root     root       6702 Apr 10 10:39  x99.conf
-rw-r--r--    1 root     root       3918 Apr 10 10:39  x99passwd.sample
```

The clients File

First, take a look at the */etc/raddb/clients* file. This file lists the hosts authorized to hit the FreeRADIUS server with requests and the secret key those hosts will use in their requests. Some common entries are already included in the */etc/raddb/clients* file, so you may wish to simply uncomment the appropriate lines. Make sure the secret key that is listed in the *clients* file is the same as that programmed into your RADIUS client equipment. Also, add the IP address of a desktop console machine with which you can test your setup using a RADIUS ping utility. A sample clients file looks like this:

```
# Client Name            Key
#---------------         ----------
#portmaster1.isp.com     testing123
#portmaster2.isp.com     testing123
#proxyradius.isp2.com    TheirKey
localhost                testing123
192.168.1.100            testing123
tc-clt.hasselltech.net   oreilly
```

 It's recommended by the FreeRADIUS developers that users move from the clients file to the *clients.conf* file. The *clients.conf* file will be addressed later in Chapter 6, but for the sake of simplicity and startup testing, I will continue using the plain clients file in this introduction.

While it may seem obvious, *change the shared secrets* from the defaults in the file or the samples listed previously. Failing to do so presents a significant security risk to your implementation and network.

The naslist File

Next, open the */etc/raddb/naslist* file. Inside this file, you should list the full canonical name of every NAS that will hit this server, its nickname, and the type of NAS.

For your test console, you can simply use the "portslave" type. Table 5-2 lists the FreeRADIUS-supported NAS equipment and the type identifier needed for the *naslist* file.

Table 5-2. Supported NAS equipment and its type identifier

NAS equipment	Type identifier
3Com/USR Hiper Arc Total Control	usrhiper
3Com/USR NetServer	netserver
3Com/USR TotalControl	tc
Ascend Max 4000 family	max40xx
Cisco Access Server family	cisco
Cistron PortSlave	portslave
Computone PowerRack	computone
Cyclades PathRAS	pathras
Livingston PortMaster	livingston
Multitech CommPlete Server	multitech
Patton 2800 family	patton

A sample */etc/raddb/naslist* file looks like this:

```
# NAS Name          Short Name    Type
#----------------    ----------    ----
#portmaster1.isp.com  pm1.NY       livingston
localhost            local         portslave
192.168.1.100        local         portslave
tc-clt.hasselltech.net  tc.char    tc
```

The naspasswd File

If you have 3Com/USR Total Control, NetServer, or Cyclades PathRAS equipment, you may need to edit the */etc/raddb/naspasswd* file. This lets the *checkrad* utility log onto your NAS machine and check to see who is logged on at what port—which is commonly used to detect multiple logins. Normally, the SNMP protocol can do this, but the equipment listed previously needs a helping hand from the *checkrad* utility. A sample */etc/raddb/naspasswd* file looks like this:

```
206.229.254.15 !root JoNAThaNHasSELl
206.229.254.5  !root FoOBaR
```

The hints File

Progressing along with the FreeRADIUS setup you will come to the */etc/raddb/hints* file. This file can be used to provide "hints" to the RADIUS server about how to provision services for a specific user based on how his login name is constructed. For example, when you've configured your default service to be a SLIP connection, then a SLIP connection will be set up if a user logs in with her standard username (e.g., *meis*). However, if that same user wanted a PPP connection, she could alter her username to be *Pmeis*, and the RADIUS server (knowing about that convention from the */etc/raddb/hints* file) would set up a PPP connection for her. Suffixes on the end of the username work in the same way. More on the hints file will be provided later in the chapter. You shouldn't need to edit this file initially since we're just testing, but if you'd like to check it out, a sample */etc/raddb/hints* file looks like this:

```
DEFAULT Prefix = "P", Strip-User-Name = Yes
        Hint = "PPP",
        Service-Type = Framed-User,
        Framed-Protocol = PPP

DEFAULT Prefix = "S", Strip-User-Name = Yes
        Hint = "SLIP",
        Service-Type = Framed-User,
        Framed-Protocol = SLIP

DEFAULT Suffix = "P", Strip-User-Name = Yes
        Hint = "PPP",
        Service-Type = Framed-User,
        Framed-Protocol = PPP

DEFAULT Suffix = "S", Strip-User-Name = Yes
        Hint = "SLIP",
        Service-Type = Framed-User,
        Framed-Protocol = SLIP
```

The huntgroups File

Let's move on to the */etc/raddb/huntgroups* file, where you define certain huntgroups. *Huntgroups* are sets of ports or other communication outlets on RADIUS client equipment. In the case of FreeRADIUS, a huntgroup can be a set of ports, a specific piece of RADIUS client equipment, or a set of calling station IDs that you want to separate from other ports.

You can filter these defined huntgroups to restrict their access to certain users and groups and match a username/password to a specific huntgroup, possibly to assign a static IP address. You define huntgroups based on the IP address of the NAS and a port range. (Keep in mind that a range can be anywhere from 1 to the maximum number of ports you have.) To configure this file, you first specify the terminal servers in each POP. Then, you configure a stanza that defines the restriction and the criteria that a potential user must satisfy to pass the restriction. That criteria is most likely a Unix username or groupname.

Again, you shouldn't have to configure this file to get basic functionality enabled for testing; if you would like to peruse the file and its features, however, I've provided a sample */etc/raddb/huntgroups* file. It's for an ISP with a POP in Raleigh, North Carolina that wants to restrict the first five ports on its second of three terminal servers in that POP to only premium customers:

```
raleigh        NAS-IP-Address == 192.168.1.101
raleigh        NAS-IP-Address == 192.168.1.102
raleigh        NAS-IP-Address == 192.168.1.103
premium        NAS-IP-Address == 192.168.1.101, NAS-Port-Id == 0-4
               Group = premium,
               Group = staff
```

The users File

FreeRADIUS allows several modifications to the original RADIUS server's style of treating users unknown to the *users* file. In the past, if a user wasn't configured in the *users* file, the server would look in the Unix password file, and then deny him access if he didn't have an account on the machine. There was only one default entry permitted. In contrast, FreeRADIUS allows multiple default entries and can "fall through" each of them to find an optimal match. The entries are processed in the order they appear in the users file, and once a match is found, RADIUS stops processing it. The Fall-Through = Yes attribute can be set to instruct the server to keep processing, even upon a match. The new FreeRADIUS *users* file can also accept spaces in the username attributes, either by escaping the space with a backslash (\) or putting the entire username inside quotation marks. Additionally, FreeRADIUS will not strip out spaces in usernames received from PortMaster equipment.

Since we won't add any users to the *users* file for our testing purposes, FreeRADIUS will fall back to accounts configured locally on the Unix machine. However, if you want to add a user to the *users* file to test that functionality, a sample */etc/raddb/users* file looks like this:

```
steve   Auth-Type := Local, User-Password == "testing"
        Service-Type = Framed-User,
        Framed-Protocol = PPP,
        Framed-IP-Address = 172.16.3.33,
        Framed-IP-Netmask = 255.255.255.0,
        Framed-Routing = Broadcast-Listen,
        Framed-Filter-Id = "std.ppp",
        Framed-MTU = 1500,
        Framed-Compression = Van-Jacobsen-TCP-IP
DEFAULT Service-Type == Framed-User
        Framed-IP-Address = 255.255.255.254,
        Framed-MTU = 576,
        Service-Type = Framed-User,
        Fall-Through = Yes
DEFAULT Framed-Protocol == PPP
        Framed-Protocol = PPP,
        Framed-Compression = Van-Jacobson-TCP-IP
```

There will be much more about the *users* file later in this chapter.

The radiusd.conf File

This file is much like Apache's *httpd.conf* file in that it lists nearly every directive and option for the basic functionality of the FreeRADIUS product. You will need to edit the Unix section of this file to make sure that the locations of the *passwd*, *shadow*, and *group* files are not commented out and are correct. FreeRADIUS needs these locations to start up. The appropriate section looks like this:

```
unix {
(some content removed)
        #  Define the locations of the normal passwd, shadow, and
        #  group files.
        #
        #  'shadow' is commented out by default, because not all
        #  systems have shadow passwords.
        #
        #  To force the module to use the system passwd fnctns,
        #  instead of reading the files, comment out the 'passwd'
        #  and 'shadow' configuration entries.  This is required
        #  for some systems, like FreeBSD.
        #
        passwd = /etc/passwd
        shadow = /etc/shadow
        group = /etc/group
(some content removed)
}
```

I will cover the *radiusd.conf* file in more detail later in this chapter.

With that done, it's now time to launch the *radiusd* daemon and test your setup. Execute *radiusd* from the command line; it should look similar to this:

```
radius:/etc/raddb # radiusd
radiusd: Starting - reading configuration files ...
radius:/etc/raddb #
```

If you receive no error messages, you now have a functional FreeRADIUS server. Congratulations!

Testing the Initial Setup

Once you have FreeRADIUS running, you need to test the configuration to make sure it is responding to requests. FreeRADIUS starts up listening, by default, on the port specified either in the local */etc/services* file or in the port directive in *radiusd. conf*. While RFC 2138 defines the standard RADIUS port to be 1812, historically RADIUS client equipment has used port 1645. Communicating via two different ports is obviously troublesome, so many users start the FreeRADIUS daemon with the -p flag, which overrides the setting in both the *letc/services* file and anything set in *radiusd.conf*. To do this, run the following from the command line:

```
radius:/etc/raddb # radiusd -p 1645
radiusd: Starting - reading configuration files ...
radius:/etc/raddb #
```

The server is now running; it is listening for and accepting requests on port 1645.

So, what is an easy way to test your configuration to see if it functions properly? It's easier than you might think, in fact. MasterSoft, Inc. has released a Windows desktop RADIUS server testing tool called NTRadPing, available at *http://www. mastersoft-group.com/download/*. The latest version as of this writing is 1.2, and it's a freeware tool. Download and install this utility on a Windows machine, and then run it. The initial application window should look much like Figure 5-1.

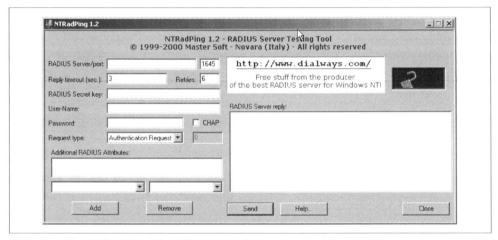

Figure 5-1. The NTRadPing 1.2 application window

To do a quick test, follow these steps:

1. Enter the IP address of your FreeRADIUS machine in the RADIUS Server/port box, and then the port number in the adjacent box. For this example, I've used IP address 192.168.1.103 and port 1645.

2. Type in the secret key you added in *letc/raddb/clients* for this Windows console machine. For this example, I used the key "testing123."

3. In the User-Name field, enter root, and in the Password field, enter the root password for your FreeRADIUS machine.

4. Select *Authentication Request* from the Request Type drop-down list box.

5. Click Send.

If your server is working properly, and you entered a valid root password, you should see the reply in the RADIUS Server reply box to the right of the NTRadPing window. You should see something like:

```
Sending authentication request to server 192.168.1.103:1645
Transmitting packet, code=1 id=1 length=47
Received response from the server in 15 milliseconds
Reply packet code=2 id=1 length=20
Response: Access-Accept
-----------------attribute dump---------------------
```

Now, change the password for root inside NTRadPing to something incorrect, and resend the request. You should get an Access-Reject message much like the one shown here:

```
Sending authentication request to server 192.168.1.103:1645
Transmitting packet, code=1 id=3 length=47
No response from server (timed out), new attempt (#1)
Received response from the server in 3516 milliseconds
Reply packet code=3 id=3 length=20
Response: Access-Reject
-----------------attribute dump---------------------
```

Next, you'll need to test accounting packets. The old standard for RADIUS accounting used port 1646. Change the port number in NTRadPing accordingly, and select *Accounting Start* from the Request Type drop-down list box. Make sure the root password is correct again, and send your request along. The response should be similar to the following:

```
Sending authentication request to server 192.168.1.103:1646
Transmitting packet, code=4 id=5 length=38
Received response from the server in 15 milliseconds
Reply packet code=5 id=5 length=20
Response: Accounting-Response
-----------------attribute dump---------------------
```

Finally, stop that accounting process by changing the Request Type box selection to *Accounting Stop* and resending the request. You should receive a response like this:

```
Sending authentication request to server 192.168.1.103:1645
Transmitting packet, code=4 id=6 length=38
Received response from the server in 16 milliseconds
Reply packet code=5 id=6 length=20
Response: Accounting-Response
-----------------attribute dump---------------------
```

If you received successful responses to all four ping tests, then FreeRADIUS is working properly. If you haven't, here's a quick list of things to check:

- Is FreeRADIUS running? Use

    ```
    ps -aux | grep radiusd
    ```
    to determine whether the process is active or not.

- Is FreeRADIUS listening on the port you're pinging? If necessary, start *radiusd* with an explicit port, i.e.,

    ```
    radiusd -p 1645
    ```

- Have you added your Windows console machine to the list of authorized clients that can hit the RADIUS server? Do this in the */etc/raddb/clients* file.

- Are you using the correct secret key? This as well is configured in the */etc/raddb/clients* file.

- Have you double-checked the locations of the *group*, *passwd*, and *shadow* files inside the *radiusd.conf* file? These locations are specified in the Unix section. Make sure they're not commented out and that the locations are correct.

- Can FreeRADIUS read the *group*, *passwd*, and *shadow* files? If you're running FreeRADIUS as root, this shouldn't be a problem, but check the permissions on these files to make sure the user/group combination under which *radiusd* is running can access those files.

- Is there any port filtering or firewalling between your console machine and the RADIUS server that is blocking communications on the ping port?

- Is the daemon taking a long time to actually start up and print a ready message (if you're running in debugging mode)? If so, your DNS configuration is broken.

To assist in diagnosing your problem, you may want to try running the server in debugging mode. While operating in this mode, FreeRADIUS outputs just about everything it does, and by simply sifting through all of the messages it prints while running, you can identify most problems.

To run the server in debugging mode, enter the following on the command line to start *radiusd*:

```
radiusd -sfxxyz -l stdout
```

It should respond with a ready message if all is well. If it doesn't, then look at the error (or errors as the case may be) and run through the checklist above.

You can also check the configuration of FreeRADIUS using the following command:

```
radiusd -c
```

This command checks the configuration of the RADIUS server and alerts you to any syntax errors in the files. It prints the status and exits with either a zero, if everything is correct, or a one if errors were present. This command is also useful when you're updating a production server that cannot be down: if there were a syntax error in the files, *radiusd* would fail to load correctly, and downtime would obviously ensue. With the check capability, this situation can be avoided.

In-depth Configuration

At this point, you've compiled, installed, configured, started, and tested a simple FreeRADIUS implementation that is functional. However, 99.5% of the RADIUS/AAA implementations around the world are just not that simple. In this section, I'll delve into the two major configuration files and discuss how to tweak, tune, customize, and effect change to the default FreeRADIUS installation. In Chapter 6, I'll discuss advanced topics, such as pluggable authentication module (PAM) support, integration with MySQL, LDAP usage, and other topics.

Configuring radiusd.conf

radiusd.conf file is the central location to configure most aspects of the FreeRADIUS product. It includes configuration directives as well as pointers and two other configuration files that may be located elsewhere on the machine. There are also general configuration options for the multitude of modules available now and in the future for FreeRADIUS. The modules can request generic options, and FreeRADIUS will pass those defined options to the module through its API.

Before we begin, some explanation is needed of the operators used in the statements and directives found in these configuration files. The = operator, as you might imagine, sets the value of an attribute. The := operator sets the value of an attribute and overwrites any previous value that was set for that attribute. The == operator compares a state with a set value. It's critical to understand how these operators work in order to obtain your desired configuration.

In this chapter, I'll look at several of the general configuration options inside *radiusd. conf*. Some of the more advanced directives in this file will be covered in Chapter 6.

pidfile

This file contains the process identification number for the *radiusd* daemon. You can use this file from the command line to perform any action to a running instance of FreeRADIUS. For example, to shut FreeRADIUS down without any protests, issue:

```
kill -9 `cat /var/run/radiusd.pid'
```

Usage: `pidfile = [path]`

Suggestion: `pidfile = ${run_dir}/radiusd.pid`

user and group

These options dictate under what user and group *radiusd* runs. It is not prudent to allow FreeRADIUS to run under a user and group with excessive permissions. In fact, to minimize the permissions granted to FreeRADIUS, use the user and group "nobody." However, on systems configured to use shadow passwords, you may need to set the user to "nobody" and the group to "shadow" so that *radiusd* can read the *shadow* file. This is not a desirable idea. On some systems, you may need to set both the user and group to "root," although it's clear why that is an even worse idea.

Usage: `user = [username]; group = [groupname]`

Suggestion: `user = nobody; group = nobody`

max_request_time

This option specifies the maximum number of seconds a request will be processed by FreeRADIUS. If the handling of a request takes longer than this threshold, the process can be killed off and an `Access-Reject` message returned. This value can range from 5 to 120 seconds.

Usage: `max_request_time = 30`

Suggestion: `max_request_time = 60`

delete_blocked_requests

This directive is paired with the `max_request_time` directive in that it controls when requests that exceed the time threshold should be killed. Most of the time, this value should be set to "no."

Usage: `delete_blocked_requests = [yes/no]`

Suggestion: `delete_blocked_requests = no`

cleanup_delay

When FreeRADIUS sends a reply to RADIUS client equipment, it generally caches that request internally for a few seconds to ensure that the RADIUS client will receive the message (sometimes network problems, offline servers, and large traffic loads might prevent the client from picking up the packet). The client receives a quick reply on its prompting for a second copy of the packet, since the internal cache mechanism for FreeRADIUS is much quicker than processing the request again. This value should be set between 2 and 10: this range is the happy medium between treating every request as a new request and caching so many processed requests that some new requests are turned away.

Usage: `cleanup_delay = [value]`

Suggestion: `cleanup_delay = 6`

max_requests

This directive specifies the maximum number of requests FreeRADIUS will keep tabs on during operation. The value starts at 256 and scales with no upper limit, and ideally this is set at the number of RADIUS clients you have multiplied by 256. Setting this value too high causes the server to eat up more system memory, while setting it too low causes a delay in processing new requests once this threshold has been met. New requests must wait for the cleanup delay period to finish before they can be serviced.

Usage: `max_requests = [value]`

Suggestion: `max_requests = [256 * x number of clients]`

bind_address

This directive specifies the address under which *radiusd* will accept requests and reply to them. The "address" can be an IP address, fully qualified domain name, or the * wildcard character (to instruct the daemon to listen on all interfaces).

Usage: `bind_address = [value]`

Suggestion: `bind_address = *`

port

This setting instructs FreeRADIUS to listen on a specific port. While the RADIUS RFC specifies that the official RADIUS port is 1812, historically NAS equipment and some RADIUS servers have used port 1645. You should be aware of the port your implementation uses. While you can specify a certain port here, you can also instruct *radiusd* to use the machine's */etc/services* file to find the port to use. Additionally, using the -p switch when executing *radiusd* will override any port setting provided here.

Usage: `port = [value]`

Suggestion: `port = 1645`

hostname_lookups

This directive tells FreeRADIUS whether to look up the canonical names of the requesting clients or simply log their IP address and move on. Much like with Apache, DNS queries take a long time and, especially on highly loaded servers, can be a detriment to performance. Turning this option on also causes *radiusd* to block the request for 30 seconds while it determines the CNAME associates with that IP address. Only turn this option on if you are sure you need it.

Usage: `hostname_lookups = [yes/no]`

Suggestion: `hostname_lookups = no`

allow_core_dumps

This directive determines whether FreeRADIUS should dump to core when it encounters an error or simply silently quit with the error. Only enable this option if you're developing for FreeRADIUS or attempting to debug a problem with the code.

Usage: allow_core_dumps = [yes/no]

Suggestion: allow_core_dumps = no

regular and extended expressions

This set of controls configures regular and extended expression support. Realistically, you shouldn't need to alter these as they're set when running the *./configure* command upon initial install.

Usage: regular_expressions = [yes/no]; extended_expressions = [yes/no]

Suggestion: regular_expressions = yes; extended expressions = yes

log

These directives control how access to and requests of the FreeRADIUS server are logged. The log_stripped_names control instructs FreeRADIUS whether to include the full User-Name attribute as it appeared in the packet. The log_auth directive specifies whether to log authentication requests or simply carry them out without logging. The log_auth_badpass control, when set to yes, causes *radiusd* to log the bad password that was attempted, while the log_auth_goodpass logs the password if it's correct.

Usage: log_stripped_names = [yes/no]; log_auth = [yes/no];
                    log_auth_badpass = [yes/no]; log_auth_goodpass = [yes/no]

Suggestion: log_stripped_names = no; log_auth = yes;
                    log_auth_badpass = yes; log_auth_goodpass = no

lower_user and lower_pass

To eliminate case problems that often plague authentication methods such as RADIUS, the FreeRADIUS developers have included a feature that will attempt to modify the User-Name and User-Password attributes to make them all lowercase; this is done either before an authentication request, after a failed authentication request using the values of the attributes as they came, or not at all.

Clearly setting the lower_user directive to after makes the most sense: it adds processing time to each request, but unless this particular machine normally carries a high load, the reduced troubleshooting time is worth the extra performance cost. However, a secure password often makes use of a combination of uppercase and lowercase letters, so security dictates leaving the password attribute alone.

| **Usage:** | `lower_user = [before/after/no]; lower_pass = [before/after/no]` |
| **Suggestion:** | `lower_user = after; lower_pass = no` |

nospace_user and nospace_pass

Much like the `lower_user` and `lower_pass` controls, these directives preprocess an Access-Request packet and ensure that no spaces are included. The available options are the same: before, after, or no. Again, the most obvious choice is to set nospace_user to after to save helpdesk time. Some administrators have a tendency to not allow spaces in passwords; if this is the case, set nospace_pass to before (since there is a system-wide policy against spaces in passwords, testing a request as-is is not required).

| **Usage:** | `nospace_user = [before/after/no]; nospace_password = [before/after/no]` |
| **Suggestion:** | `nospace_user = after; nospace_password = before` |

Configuring the users File

The *users* file, located at */etc/raddb/users*, is the home of all authentication security information for each user configured to access the system. Each user has an individual stanza, or entry. The file has a standard format for each stanza:

1. The first field is the username for each user, up to 253 characters.

2. On the same line, the next criteria are a list of required authentication attributes such as protocol type, password, and port number.

3. Following the first line, each user has a set of defined characteristics that allow FreeRADIUS to provision a service best for that user. These characteristics are indented under the first line and separated into one characteristic per line. For example, you might find a Login-Host entry, a dial-back configuration, or perhaps PPP configuration information.

The *users* file also comes with a default username of—you guessed it—DEFAULT, which is generally the catchall configuration. That is to say, if there is no explicit match for a particular user, or perhaps the attribute information for a user is incomplete, *radiusd* will configure the session based on the information in the DEFAULT entry.

FreeRADIUS processes this file in the order in which the entries are listed. When information received from the RADIUS client equipment matches an entry in the *users* file, FreeRADIUS stops processing and sets the service up based on that *users* file entry. However, you can alter this behavior by setting the Fall-Through attribute to yes in an entry. When *radiusd* encounters a positive fall-through entry, it will continue processing the *users* file and then select the best match for the particular session. The DEFAULT user can also have a Fall-Through attribute, which means you can have multiple DEFAULT entries for various connection scenarios.

If you don't want to issue a password for each user via their entry in the *users* file, then simply set Auth-Type := System on the first line for each user. FreeRADIUS will then query the system password database for the correct password, which saves some administrative headache.

A sample complete entry

The following is a complete entry for the user *jhassell*, dialing into a NAS server using PPP. Note that (a) there is no Fall-Through attribute set, so FreeRADIUS will stop processing when it encounters this entry, and (b) no DEFAULT entry will be used to add attribute information to this connection:

```
jhassell    Auth-Type := System
            Service-Type = Framed-User,
            Framed-Protocol = PPP,
            Framed-IP-Address = 192.168.1.152,
            Framed-IP-Netmask = 255.255.255.0,
            Framed-Routing = Broadcast-Listen,
            Framed-Filter-Id = "20modun",
            Framed-MTU = 1500,
            Framed-Compression = Van-Jacobsen-TCP-IP
```

Next, here's a complete entry for the user Anna Watson. She has a space in her username and she also has a password specified in her entry. She also gets a positive fall-through so that she can use some of the DEFAULT user's attributes with her connection:

```
"Anna Watson"    Auth-Type := Local, User-Password == "yes123"
                 Reply-Message = "Hello, %u"
                 Service-Type = Framed-User,
                 Framed-Routing = Broadcast-Listen,
                 Framed-Filter-Id = "20modun",
                 Fall-Through = Yes
```

DEFAULT entries

These DEFAULT user configurations match with all usernames that can get to them (i.e., the individual users must have a positive Fall-Through attribute). Recall from the earlier discussion that DEFAULT entries may also have Fall-Through attributes.

First, let's make sure that all users are checked against the system password file unless they have a password explicitly assigned in the entry.

```
DEFAULT    Auth-Type := System
           Fall-Through = Yes
```

Now, include a DEFAULT entry for all users connecting via a framed protocol, such as PPP or SLIP. Note that I tell the RADIUS client to assign the IP address via the Framed-IP-Address attribute's value (see Chapter 3 for details).

```
DEFAULT    Service-Type = Framed-User
           Framed-IP-Address = 255.255.255.254,
           Framed-MTU = 576,
           Service-Type = Framed-User,
           Fall-Through = Yes
```

Finally, set the DEFAULT entry for PPP users. I've already told FreeRADIUS to assign framed protocol users with a dynamic IP address, so all I need to do is set the compression method and explicitly designate PPP as the framed protocol for this default.

```
DEFAULT    Framed-Protocol == PPP
           Framed-Protocol = PPP,
           Framed-Compression = Van-Jacobsen-TCP-IP
```

If a user attempts to connect and matches neither any of the explicit user entries nor any of the DEFAULT entries, then he will be denied access. Notice that with the last DEFAULT entry, Fall-Through isn't set: this ensures the user is kicked off if he doesn't match any of the scenarios.

Prefixes and suffixes

You can use prefixes and suffixes appended to the user name to determine what kind of service to provision for that particular connection. For example, if a user adds *.shell* to their username, you add the following DEFAULT entry to the users file to provision a shell service for her. FreeRADIUS authenticates her against the system password file, telnets to your shell account machine, and logs her in.

```
DEFAULT    Suffix == ".shell", Auth-Type := System
           Service-Type = Login-User,
           Login-Service = Telnet,
           Login-IP-Host = shellacct1.rduinternet.com
```

Similarly, you can set up an entry in the users file where if a user connects with a prefix of "s.", then you can provision SLIP service for him. FreeRADIUS can authenticate him against the system passwords, and then fall through to pick up the SLIP attributes from another DEFAULT entry. Here is an example:

```
DEFAULT    Prefix == "s.", Auth-Type := System
           Service-Type = Framed-User,
           Framed-Protocol = SLIP,
           Fall-Through = Yes
```

Using RADIUS callback

The callback feature of the RADIUS protocol is one of the most interesting and useful security measures that you, as an administrator, can enforce. You can configure FreeRADIUS to call a specific user back via his individual entry in the users file. (Of course, you could make a DEFAULT entry that calls every user back, but the application of that technique is more limited and requires many more resources than a standard implementation.) The following is an example of a callback configuration for user *rneis*: she dials in, is then called back, is authenticated, and then given a session on the shell account machine.

```
rneis    Auth-Type := System
         Service-Type = Callback-Login-User,
         Login-Service = Telnet,
         Login-IP-Host = shellacct1.rduinternet.com,
         Callback-Number = "9,1-919-555-1212"
```

Completely denying access to users

You can set up a specific user entry to deny access to him. For example, you may have an automated script that takes input from your billing system (a list of usernames that have not paid their bills, possibly) and re-writes user entries to deny access. They would write something like the following, for the user *aslyter*:

```
aslyter   Auth-Type := Reject
          Reply-Message = "Account disabled for nonpayment."
```

Alternatively, you could also set up a group on your system called "suspended," and FreeRADIUS could detect whether an individual username was contained within that group and reject access as necessary. To do this, create a DEFAULT entry much like the following:

```
DEFAULT   Group == "suspended", Auth-Type := Reject
          Reply-Message = "Account suspended for late payment."
```

Troubleshooting Common Problems

In this section, I'll take a look at some of the most frequently occurring problems with a new FreeRADIUS setup and how to fix them.

Linking Errors When Starting FreeRADIUS

If you receive an error similar to the following:

```
Module: Loaded SQL
rlm_sql: Could not link driver rlm_sql_mysql: file not found
rlm_sql: Make sure it (and all its depend libraries!) are in the search path
radiusd.conf[50]: sql: Module instantiation failed.
```

It means that some shared libraries on the server are not available. There are a couple of possible causes from this.

First, the libraries that are needed by the module listed in the error messages couldn't be found when FreeRADIUS was being compiled. However, if a static version of the module was available, it was built at compile time. This would have been indicated with very prominent messages at compile time.

The other cause is that the dynamic linker on your server is not configured correctly. This would result in the libraries that are required being found at compile time, but not run time. FreeRADIUS makes use of standard calls to link to these shared libraries, so if these calls fail, the system is misconfigured. This can be fixed by telling the linker where these libraries are on your system, which can be done in one of the following ways:

- Write a script that starts FreeRADIUS and includes the variable *LD_LIBRARY_ PATH*. This sets the paths where these libraries can be found.

- If your system allows it, edit the */etc/ld.so.conf* file and add the directory containing the shared libraries to the list.

- Set the path to these libraries inside *radiusd.conf* using the *libdir* configuration directive. The *radiusd.conf* file has more details on this.

Incoming Request Passwords Are Gibberish

Gibberish is usually indicative of an incorrectly formed or mismatched shared secret, the phrase shared between the server and the RADIUS client machine and used to perform secure encryption on packets. To identify the problem, run the server in debugging mode, as described previously. The first password printed to the console screen will be inside a RADIUS attribute (e.g., Password = "rneis\dfkjdf7482odf") and the second will be in a logged message (e.g., Login failed [rneis/ dfkjdf7482odf]). If the data after the slash is gibberish—ensure it's not just a really secure password—then the shared secret is not consistent between the server and the RADIUS client. This may even be due to hidden characters, so to be completely sure both are the same, delete and re-enter the secret on both machines.

The gibberish may also result from a shared secret that is too long. FreeRADIUS limits the secret length to 16 characters, since some NAS equipment has limitations on the length of the secret yet don't make it evident in error logs or the documentation.

NAS Machine Ignores a RADIUS Reply

You may be seeing duplicate accounting or authentication requests without accompanying successful user logins. In this case, it's likely that you have a multi-homed RADIUS server, or at least a server with multiple IP addresses. If the server receives a request on one IP address, but responds with a different one, even if the reply comes from the machine for which the original packet was destined, the NAS machine will not accept it. To rectify this, launch FreeRADIUS with the -i command-line switch, which binds the daemon to one specific IP address.

CHAP Authentication Doesn't Work Correctly

If PAP authentication works normally, but users authenticating with the CHAP protocol receive errors and denials, you do not have plain text passwords in the users file. CHAP requires this, while PAP can take passwords from the system or from any other source. For each user who needs CHAP authentication, you must add the Password = changeme check item to his individual entry, of course changing the value of the password as appropriate.

Some people may say using CHAP is much more secure, since the user passwords are not transmitted in plain text over the connection between the user and the NAS. This is simply not true in practice. While hiding the password during transmission is beneficial, the CHAP protocol requires you to leave plain text passwords sitting in a file on a server, completely unencrypted. Obviously, it's much more likely that a cracker will gain access to your RADIUS server, grab the *users* file with all of these plainly available passwords, and wreak havoc and harm on your network than it is that the same cracker would intercept *one* user's password during the establishment of the connection.

## CHAPTER 6

Advanced FreeRADIUS

Congratulations! Chances are that, by now, you have a base FreeRADIUS system up, running, and tested to be working correctly. But it's probably not an optimal system for your implementation and needs. In this chapter, I'll take a look at some of the more advanced tools and methods you can use to extend the capabilities of FreeRADIUS and better integrate it with your existing environment.

Using PAM

FreeRADIUS supports the pluggable authentication model, or PAM, but that must be enabled at compile time. (A discussion of PAM is beyond the scope of this book; however, an excellent introduction to PAM, with answers to some frequently asked questions, is available at *http://www.kernel.org/pub/linux/libs/pam/FAQ.*) However, the current support for PAM is rather non-standard. In most RADIUS distributions, to enable PAM in transactions, enter User-Password = PAM in the *users* file; this is not supported in FreeRADIUS. You must instead use Auth-Type = Pam. For example, here is a configuration stanza for a non-specific (that is to say, default) user configured for PAM authentication, when he logs in from a specific RADIUS client machine:

```
DEFAULT Auth-Type := Pam, NAS-IP-Address == 206.229.254.5
    Service-Type = Framed-User,
    Framed-Protocol = PPP,
    Framed-IP-Address = 255.255.255.254,
    Filter-Id = "20modun",
    Framed-MTU = 1500,
    Framed-Compression = Van-Jacobson-TCP-IP
```

In some configurations, you may have specific entries configured in the */etc/pam.d* file. The following *users* file configuration stanza uses a unique "Pam-Auth = x" identifier to direct the RADIUS server to a specific *pam.d* entry. FreeRADIUS defaults this string to RADIUS:

```
DEFAULT Auth-Type := Pam, Pam-Auth == "hasselltech-radius", NAS-IP-Address == 127.0.0.1
    Service-Type = Framed-User,
```

```
            Framed-Protocol = PPP,
            Framed-IP-Address = 255.255.255.254,
            Filter-Id = "15intonly",
            Framed-MTU = 1500,
            Framed-Compression = Van-Jacobson-TCP-IP
```

Ensure that your compiler's settings are configured to enable PAM support when you first begin your FreeRADIUS installation.

Open your *radiusd.conf* file and scroll to the modules section. Enable PAM functionality by examining the *pam* section inside the modules divider. The value for the *pam_auth* string corresponds with a file in the */etc/pam.d* directory on your system. Enter a name here, and make a note of it, as shown in this example:

```
    pam {
                #
                #  The name to use for PAM authentication.
                #  PAM looks in /etc/pam.d/${pam_auth_name}
                #  for its configuration.  See 'redhat/radiusd-pam'
                #  for a sample PAM configuration file.
                #
                #  Note that any Pam-Auth attribute set in the 'users'
                #  file overrides this one.
                #
                pam_auth = radiusd
    }
```

In the same file, scroll down to the authentication section and make sure the *pam* line is not commented out:

```
    authenticate {
            pam
            unix
    #       ldap
    #       mschap
    #       eap
    }
```

Now, navigate to the */etc/pam.d* directory on your system and create a file with the same name you specified in the *pam* section inside *radiusd.conf*. (In the previous example, I used *radiusd*.) Insert the following lines into this new file:

```
    #%PAM-1.0
    auth        required    /lib/security/pam_unix_auth.so shadow md5 nullok
    auth        required    /lib/security/pam_nologin.so
    account     required    /lib/security/pam_unix_acct.so
    password    required    /lib/security/pam_cracklib.so
    password    required    /lib/security/pam_unix_passwd.so shadow md5 nullok use_
    authtok
    session     required    /lib/security/pam_unix_session.so
```

You may wish to change some of these settings to suit your specific configuration, but those default strings will work for most any implementation. Next, make sure that the group under which the *radiusd* process is running can read the */etc/shadow* file. Unless you're running as root, PAM won't be able to read the file otherwise and will subsequently malfunction. You also need to specify the user and group with read permissions to */etc/shadow* in the *radiusd.conf* file.

Proxying and Realms

FreeRADIUS can act as a proxy server that adheres to the RFC specifications. To use realms, a user will likely dial in with a preferred syntax as discussed in Chapter 2: commonly, this is in the format of *user@realm* or *realm/user*. To configure the proper syntax for your implementation, consult the realm module configuration section of the *radiusd.conf* file (in the */etc/raddb* directory).

Further realm configuration takes place in the */etc/raddb/proxy.conf* file. There is also another file, */etc/raddb/realms*, but the developers of FreeRADIUS suggest using the more expandable and functional *proxy.conf* file for this purpose. The *proxy.conf* file lists various settings and configuration directives for the proxy functionality, as well as a realm configuration section in which you detail which realms belong to which authentication hosts. For example, for the realm *ralint*, the following entry would be added to the *proxy.conf* file:

```
realm ralint {
    type      = radius
    authhost  = radius.raleighinternet.com:1645
    accthost  = radius.raleighinternet.com:1646
    secret    = triangle
    nostrip
}
```

You can also configure local realms whose authentication requests are not proxied. In this case, you don't need to list a secret in the configuration. For instance:

```
realm durhamnet {
    type= radius
    authhost= LOCAL
    accthost= LOCAL
}
```

A *NULL* realm can be used for authentication requests without a realm specified. A NULL entry might look something like this:

```
realm NULL {
    type= radius
    authhost= radius.raleighinternet.com:1645
    accthost= radius.raleighinternet.com:1646
    secret= triangle
}
```

Finally, much like in the *users* file, there can be a DEFAULT entry that will apply to all other realms not explicitly matched. Here is an example:

```
realm DEFAULT {
    type= radius
    authhost= radlocal.corp.raleighinternet.com:1645
    accthost= radlocal.corp.raleighinternet.com:1646
    secret= iamnotamicrosoftmachine
}
```

There exist several more options with which you can configure proxying and realm functionality in the *proxy.conf* file. Table 6-1 lists the options.

Table 6-1. Realm and proxy configuration options

Option	Description
nostrip	This instructs FreeRADIUS not to strip the realm prefix or suffix before proxying a request. The default is to strip the realm identifier.
hints	This tells *radiusd* to send the username to the remote RADIUS server after the local hints file has been processed. The default is to send the original User-Name attribute unaltered.
notrealm	This option overrides the default action to proxy a user who logs on with a User-Name attribute that matches a defined realm.

Using the clients.conf File

In Chapter 5, I configured a very basic FreeRADIUS system using the plain-vanilla *clients* file. That file is obsolesced by the more flexible *clients.conf* file. It's very simple to configure, however.

There are two types of entries in the *clients.conf* file: clients and NASes, or more generally, RADIUS client equipment. Clients are standard requestors used in most authentication scenarios. In the case of a client entry, the canonical name or IP address of the original source request will be matched to an entry in the *clients.conf* file, and the secret will be compared to verify the integrity of the request. A NAS entry is used for all RADIUS client equipment where it's actually a NAS or another type of client. The NAS entry changes the criteria by which request information is compared to an entry: NAS entries use the NAS-IP-Address attribute in the original source request to match the appropriate entry and then progress to the NAS-Ident attribute.

A sample complete *clients.conf* entry shown here:

```
client 172.16.1.55 {
    secret     = donttellanyone
    shortname  = totalcontrol
    vendor     = 3comusr
    type       = tc
    login      = !root
    password   = changeme
```

```
nas 172.16.1.66 {
    secret      = iamanas
    shortname   = max6000
    vendor      = lucent
    type        = ascend
    login       = !root
    password    = changeme
```

FreeRADIUS with Some NAS Gear

For a variety of reasons, vendors have been known to not adhere to RFC specifications. Often their products are based on an early draft of a proposed specification, sometimes vendors fail to update their products to the revised guidelines, and sometimes vendors simply choose to ignore the specification entirely. In any case, as an administrator you must cope. Unfortunately, the concept of vendor-specific irregularities and peculiarities is not foreign to NAS gear.

This section is designed to at least familiarize you with the vagaries of using some models of terminal server equipment with FreeRADIUS. Wherever possible, I will offer a workaround, another option, or some other recommendation to assist you in compensating for the problem.

Ascend Equipment

Traditionally, the attributes specific to Ascend terminal server gear are sent by FreeRADIUS as vendor-specific attributes, as per the RADIUS RFC. However, the Ascend NAS equipment itself sends its own attributes (those that are specific to the Ascend equipment) as regular, global space attributes, which, of course, causes problems with other attributes as specified in the RFC. If you suffer from a problem related to Ascend's non-standard way of dealing with its specific attributes, you will see invalid Message-Authenticator messages in your log files.

There are two options to fix this problem. The first is to enable support for vendor-specific attributes on the Ascend equipment. There are different steps to follow depending on which model of terminal server you have. If your model is the Max6000 or Max4000 series with the menu-style TAOS interface, follow these instructions:

1. Go to Ethernet, select *Mod Config*, and then choose *Auth*.

2. Find the *Auth-Compat* option at the bottom of the menu. Change this from its current setting, *OLD*, to *VSA*.

3. Save the change to make it active.

If you have the Max TNT model or the Apex 8000 series with the command-line–driven TAOS system, execute the following commands from a shell prompt.

```
nas> read external-auth
nas> set rad-auth-client auth-radius-compat = vendor-specific
nas> set rad-acct-client acct-radius-compat = vendor-specific
nas> write
```

The other option is to perform the opposite change: enable the *old* attributes on the FreeRADIUS machine. This is a bit easier to do, since all that is required is preceding the Ascend attributes with *X-* wherever they're found. For example, the vendor-specific attribute Ascend-Data-Filter would become, in old-style attribute naming, X-Ascend-Data-Filter. It's worth noting that some Cisco equipment has the capability to emulate Ascend NAS gear with 100% compatibility, so consider whether you have mixed gear when choosing the option to rid yourself of the Ascend integration problems.

Cisco Equipment

Cisco equipment runs the IOS software and, while it's become a common piece of equipment to find in an ISP, it does have some quirks of its own. Let's take a look at a few.

If you are running IOS Version 12 (either the .0 or .1 releases), then set the following configuration commands:

```
aaa new-model
aaa authentication login default group radius local
aaa authentication login localauth local
aaa authentication ppp default if-needed group radius local
aaa authorization exec default group radius local
aaa authorization network default group radius local
aaa accounting delay-start
aaa accounting exec default start-stop group radius
aaa accounting network default start-stop group radius
aaa processes 6
```

If you are running IOS Version 11.1, then set the following configuration commands:

```
aaa new-model
aaa authentication ppp radppp if-needed radius
aaa authorization network radius none
aaa accounting network wait-start radius
aaa accounting network wait radius
radius-server timeout 3
```

This instructs the NAS to communicate with a RADIUS server and eliminates a lot of duplicate log entries. If you run IOS Version 11.3, then add the following command to the previous list:

```
aaa accounting update newinfo
```

This allows the IP address assigned to the user to be displayed upon running the *radwho* program (discussed earlier in the chapter). By default, the default Accounting

Start packet sent from the NAS doesn't include the new client's IP address. This command tells IOS to send another packet that updates the accounting records with the client's IP address when it is assigned.

 Perhaps the most critical of these new settings is the aaa accounting delay-start attribute. This directive tells the NAS equipment not to send the Accounting Start packet until the client has received an IP address. This eliminates some of the lag problems found with IOS Version 11 equipment and the need to send IP address updates (known as "alive" packets) to the RADIUS server during the negotiation process. By using the configuration settings above, the FreeRADIUS machine will authenticate all requests for Telnet sessions automatically. To gain access to a terminal server itself that is running IOS 12, you need to create an entry in the *users* file similar to this (you may change either the username or password; they are not required to be as they are in this example):

```
!superuserUser-Password == "ciscoios"
            Service-Type = NAS-Prompt-User
```

This will grant you access. You will still need to use your secret in conjunction with the enable command to perform high-level configuration modification.

Nortel Equipment

All Nortel equipment using the Bay software with a revision prior to Version 18.0.2 must upgrade to at least that version. There is a bug in the encoding of the secret passed between the RADIUS server, the NAS gear, and the client: versions prior to the desired revision pass a secret that is encoded purely with MD5, while the RADIUS RFC requires it differently. You will know if you have this problem if you have log file messages relating to invalid Message-Authenticators.

3Com and US Robotics Equipment

You may see the following error entry in your log files if you use HiPerArc 4.1.11 equipment from 3Com/US Robotics:

```
Wed Jun 19 14:50:32 2002: Error: Accounting: logout: entry for NAS tc-if5 port 1 has
wrong ID
```

The software has a hard time telling FreeRADIUS about its port numbers. The manufacturer has updated firmware available at *http://totalservice.usr.com*, which you should install immediately. If you're outside the United States, call the Global Response Center at (800) 879489, and they'll assist you with the upgrade.

Using MySQL with FreeRADIUS

Many FreeRADIUS users have been toying with interacting *radiusd* with MySQL, which is a wonderful open source database product. Using a database allows the administrator to query data and produce reports after transactions are complete using a standard language, SQL, which is supported across platforms. Also, a database allows users and passwords to be kept in a central place, and other services can access it and make said database an extensible, complete resource. Additionally, it's a centralized administration point, which reduces the administrative headache of offering a service to the public. This section describes one possible setup to allow FreeRADIUS to authenticate against a user database held inside MySQL.

By using MySQL, you put the contents of the *users* file inside the database, and instead of storing all of the user information in one file, with separate stanzas for each user, the data will now exist in several different database tables. This majorly improves speed and scalability and offers a modicum of flexibility, too.

First, download, compile, and install MySQL for your RADIUS machine. There are several web resources available to assist you in doing this:

- The MySQL web site (*http://www.mysql.com*) offers database downloads as well as API information, graphical tools to manage the database, applications contributed by third parties, and complete documentation for the core database product.

- There is also a convenient Windows-based tool to manage a remote MySQL database called SQLion (*http://www.exxatools.com/SQLion.html*) that will make it easy to create and populate tables. Of course, in lieu of a desktop-based product, there is also the venerable Linux tool, *phpMyAdmin* (*http://www.phpwizard. net/projects/phpMyAdmin/*), which can be used over the Web for much the same purpose.

> It is imperative that you have the *mysql-devel* package installed (with headers and libraries included) before compiling and installing FreeRADIUS. If you don't, *radiusd* will not compile with MySQL support properly.

To begin the rest, follow these steps:

1. Download, compile, and install FreeRADIUS. This process is detailed in Chapter 5. Using MySQL in conjunction with *radiusd* doesn't call for any special compile-time or install-time flags, so a vanilla installation should function correctly.

2. Configure the test RADIUS system, also as described in Chapter 5. You will want to add a user in the shell (use the useradd command) to use for authentication purposes. The remainder of this section will assume you created a user "radius" in the system that belongs to a group "radius."

3. Test the setup using the NTRadPing utility, as described in Chapter 5.

 Some users have noted that NTRadPing operates correctly using test authentication requests and replies but completely ignores or malfunctions when sending accounting packets of any type. This is because the accounting process needs the Acct-Session-Time attribute to properly account for the packet. In NTRadPing, ensure you add that attribute (with a value of 9999, perhaps) before sending the accounting stop and start packets.

At this point, your RADIUS setup should respond correctly to test requests. The authentication information is being retrieved from and compared against data in text files. Now let's add MySQL to the fray.

Once MySQL is installed, create the schema for your user database. There exists within the standard FreeRADIUS distribution a command script file that will easily create a SQL database and populate it with the necessary fields. Of course, you can create your own database schema, but for the purposes of this tutorial, I'll assume that you've used the schema creation script included with the FreeRADIUS distribution. You can find this script, *db_mysql.sql*, in the *{unpacked}/src/modules/rlm_sql/ drivers/rlm_sql_mysql* directory, where *{unpacked}* is the location in your file system where the unpacked distribution files reside.

There are several ways to run this script. Perhaps the simplest way is to run the script locally on the RADIUS machine from the shell using this command:

```
mysql -u{root} -p{rootpass} radius < db_mysql.sql
```

where **{root}** is the root user or a specific username you've configured for the RADIUS/MySQL interaction, and **{rootpass}** is that user's password. Make sure to leave off the curly braces; they are added only for clarification. Also note that there is no space between the flag and the data. You can also use the database management tools described earlier; to execute the SQL script, consult the individual product's documentation.

Next, instruct FreeRADIUS that you intend to use SQL for all RADIUS functions. Open */etc/raddb/radiusd.conf* in your favorite text editor and make the following changes:

1. Add sql to the *authorize* section, between the *suffix* and *files* entries.

2. In the *accounting* section, between *unix* and *radutmp*, add sql to the mix.

Examples 6-1 and 6-2 illustrate what the final modifications to the *radiusd.conf* file should look like.

Example 6-1. The "authorize" section

```
authorize {
        preprocess
#       counter
#       attr_filter
#       eap
        suffix
        sql
        files
#       mschap
}
```

Example 6-2. The "accounting" section

```
accounting {
#       acct_unique
        detail
#       counter
        unix
        sql
        radutmp
#       sradutmp
}
```

Next, add the username and password you configured for the MySQL user database (if you've been following the examples to the letter, I've simply used the root user) to */etc/raddb/sql.conf*. You can leave the rest of the file alone if you used the automated script to create the database schema. You may want to turn *sqltrace* on to see the various communications between *radiusd* and MySQL. The following reflects these modifications to *sql.conf*:

```
sql {

# Database type
# Current supported are: rlm_sql_mysql, rlm_sql_postgresql,
# rlm_sql_iodbc, rlm_sql_oracle, rlm_sql_unixodbc
driver = "rlm_sql_mysql"

# Connect info
server = "localhost"
login = "root"
password = "rootpass"

# Database table configuration
radius_db = "radius"

# If you want both stop and start records logged to the
# same SQL table, leave this as is.  If you want them in
# different tables, put the start table in acct_table1
# and stop table in acct_table2
acct_table1 = "radacct"
acct_table2 = "radacct"
```

```
authcheck_table = "radcheck"
authreply_table = "radreply"

groupcheck_table = "radgroupcheck"
groupreply_table = "radgroupreply"

usergroup_table = "usergroup"

# Remove stale session if checkrad does not see a double login
deletestalesessions = yes

# Print all SQL statements when in debug mode (-x)
sqltrace = yes
sqltracefile = ${logdir}/sqltrace.sql
```

 Despite the previous example, avoid placing your root username and password in the file. I included it above for the sake of simplicity while testing the configuration. Before moving a new database into production, add a non-privileged account and use that login information in this file.

The configuration is almost complete. For any testing of the new database setup to work, you need to add user information so that there is data to authenticate against. Follow these steps to add some general user information with which to test.

1. In the *usergroup* table, create entries matching user account names to group names.

2. In the *radcheck* table, create entries for each of the usernames you created in Step 1 and specify their passwords in the Password attribute.

3. In the *radreply* table, match the usernames to the specific attributes to be returned when FreeRADIUS replies to an authentication request.

4. Finally, inside the *radgroupreply*, create replies to be matched when requests are made from users inside certain groups. (This step is optional: I will continue with it in this example to demonstrate the functionality, but for simple setups nothing is needed in this table for the database authentication to work properly.)

Tables 6-2, 6-3, 6-4, and 6-5 show some sample data for your new user database.

Table 6-2. Usergroup

ID	UserName	GroupName
1	Jhassell	Dialin
2	Rneis	Staticdial
3	Bgrossman	Suspended
4	Awatson	dialin

Table 6-3. Radcheck

ID	UserName	Attribute	Value	Op
1	Jhassell	Password	Changeme	==
2	Rneis	Password	Thewb	==
3	Bgrossman	Password	Sarah	==
4	Awatson	Password	Moo	==

Table 6-4. Radreply

ID	UserName	Attribute	Value
1	Rneis	Framed-IP-Address	66.26.224.46
2	Bgrossman	Auth-Type	Reject

Table 6-5. Radgroupreply

ID	GroupName	Attribute	Value	Op
34	Dialin	Framed-Compression	Van-Jacobsen-TCP-IP	==
33	Dialin	Framed-Protocol	PPP	==
32	Dialin	Service-Type	Framed-User	==
31	Dialin	Auth-Type	Local	:=
35	Dialin	Framed-MTU	1500	==
36	Staticdialin	Auth-Type	Local	:=
37	Staticdialin	Framed-Protocol	PPP	==
38	Staticdialin	Service-Type	Framed-User	==
39	Staticdialin	Framed-Compression	Van-Jacobsen-TCP-IP	==

With the configuration now complete, restart FreeRADIUS and test your setup using the instructions for using NTRadPing in Chapter 5. Test each of your usernames and ensure that the proper attributes are returned as they're configured in the *radreply* and *radgroupreply* tables.

Extending the MySQL Functionality

Now that the basic MySQL support has been installed, configured, and tested, this section will help you enable more advanced features that extend the capabilities of the FreeRADIUS/MySQL combination.

Realm support

It is fairly simple to get realm support when using the database model for FreeRADIUS authentication. You need to enable the stripped usernames feature of FreeRADIUS in order for realm support to work. If not, FreeRADIUS passes the full value of the username attribute—*jhassell@raleighinternet*, for example—and, in this case, the database is not set up to support that. By enabling stripped usernames, FreeRADIUS deletes the *@raleighinternet* portion of the username, which allows the query against the database to proceed successfully.

To enable the stripped user name functionality:

1. Open */etc/raddb/sql.conf* in your favorite text editor.
2. Locate the section called *query config: username*.
3. Uncomment the line *sql_user_name = "%{Stripped-User-Name:-%{User-Name:-none}}";*
4. Comment out the line *sql_user_name = "%{User-Name}"*

The realm functionality should work as expected. If you, in fact, do need to distinguish users in your database (only if your usernames are *not* unique across all realms), then edit the user entries inside the authentication database and disable the realm-stripping feature.

Redundancy with MySQL

To introduce a level of fault tolerance and added data integrity security, you may want to consider having two machines running MySQL that replicate the user authentication database between themselves. While it's certainly not a customized high-availability scenario like that covered in Chapter 10, it is a relatively inexpensive and functional way to ensure that some type of contingency plan covers your customers.

To begin, make sure you have two machines running exactly the same version and revision of MySQL. This reduces the complexity of the entire setup and makes it easier to troubleshoot should something go wrong. Determine which machine will act as the master server and which will act as slave (there really is no significance to which machine you select other than the push direction of the replication).

Next, copy the database directories as a set over to the slave machine to ensure both machines already have the databases. Change the ownership of the newly copied directories on the slave machine by executing the following:

```
chown -R mysql:mysql /path/to/data/directories
```

You may want to use the *mysqldump* utility instead to "dump" a copy of the database from the master server to the slave machine—this approach works best if the two servers are running different operating systems. Then open up */etc/my.cnf* (or create it if it doesn't exist) on the master server and add the following lines:

```
[mysqld]
socket=/tmp/mysql.sock
server-id=1
log-bin
```

Replace */tmp/mysql.sock* with the path to your *mysql.sock* file if it's not located in */tmp*.

Finally, grant permission for the slave server to connect and replicate the master server's database by running the following SQL command (where *x.x.x.x* is the IP address of your slave server and password is a password of your choosing that the slave server will be configured to use):

```
GRANT FILE ON *.* TO replicate@x.x.x.x IDENTIFIED BY 'password';
```

Kill the MySQL daemon on the master machine, restart it, and then ensure everything still works as it did before.

Now it's time to configure the slave server. Open */etc/my.cnf* (or create it if it doesn't exist) on the slave server and add the following lines:

```
[mysqld]
socket=/tmp/mysql.sock
server-id=2
master-host=x.x.x.x
master-user=replicate
master-password=password
```

Replace */tmp/mysql.sock* with the path to your *mysql.sock* file if it's not located in */tmp*. Also note that the server-id value must be different than the master computer's ID, and that the master-password value is what you configured in the previous SQL statement that was executed on the master server. Next, kill the MySQL daemon on the slave machine, restart it, and then ensure everything still works as it did before.

Finally, execute the following SQL command to see if the replication is working:

```
SHOW SLAVE STATUS;
```

You should see a message indicating the procedure was successful. To test whether the replication functionality is indeed working, change some data on the master—for instance, change a password for a user in the *radcheck* table. Then query that same record on the slave machine: it should reflect the change, since the replication is instantaneous.

Simultaneous Use

Recall from Chapter 1 that RADIUS is a stateless protocol. Additionally, because of the way RADIUS accounting works, it's entirely possible and even probable that a RADIUS server will have an internal list of who is currently logged on that is different than the actual state of the RADIUS client ports—in other words, your RADIUS server may think users are logged on when they really aren't, and vice versa. Fortunately, most NAS equipment includes some mechanism by which the administrator (or the RADIUS daemon servicing authentication requests) can query it to find out which user is assigned to what port. This could be done through Telnet, the deprecated finger protocol, or even the Simple Network Monitoring Protocol (SNMP).

This ability is especially important when attempting to control multiple logins at the same time from the same user. There exists a utility to tell FreeRADIUS to check on the terminal server first to see if a user is already logged on before denying his request to log on, thereby compensating for the RADIUS accounting discrepancies. The best way to do this is by installing two modules—the *SNMP_Session* and BER modules—from the popular traffic-monitoring program MRTG. (These are core Perl modules, actually.) Having those modules installed lets a utility included in FreeRADIUS, the *checkrad* script, communicate with the terminal server equipment directly using the SNMP protocol. You can obtain more information and download these modules from the "SNMP Support for Perl 5" web site at *http://www.switch.ch/misc/leinen/snmp/perl/*.

 If you have USR/3Com Total Control terminal server gear and you want to make use of the checking routine, you will need the Net:: Telnet module for Perl 5. This can be obtained from the CPAN archive at *http://www.perl.com/CPAN/*.

To enforce a simultaneous-use restriction, you need to add a parameter to either an individual user's entry or a DEFAULT entry in the RADIUS *users* file (*/etc/raddb/users*). The value of the Simultaneous-Use attribute is the number of sessions that can occur at the same time with the same username. To enforce a restriction on user *awatson*, for example, of two simultaneous connections, I would configure a user entry for her similar to the following:

```
Awatson     Auth-Type := System, Simultaneous-Use := 2
            Service-Type = Framed User
            <continue attribute listing>
```

You can also define a certain group of users—for example, a multilink group that can have two logins concurrently—while the rest of the user base can only have one simultaneous session. To achieve this, use the following DEFAULT entries and the fall-through feature:

```
DEFAULT     Group == "multilink", Simultaneous-Use := 2
            Fall-Through = 1
DEFAULT     Simultaneous-Use = 1
            Fall-Through = 1
```

Once this is configured, the server now knows to use the *checkrad* script (located at either */usr/local/sbin/checkrad* or */usr/sbin/checkrad*). When does it invoke the script? When a user connects, FreeRADIUS looks in its list of currently active users, which is kept in */var/log/radutmp*. (Executing *radwho* at a command prompt will display the contents of this file on the screen.) If it finds that the username associated with the pending request is already listed in *radutmp*, then it will execute the *checkrad* script. The *checkrad* script then communicates with the NAS gear via finger, Telnet, or SNMP and determines whether that user is indeed logged on. It then either accepts or denies the request for a concurrent session based on the value of the Simultaneous-Use attribute as configured in the *users* file.

Be forewarned that the load and performance impact of using *checkrad* can be quite significant and can affect not only the RADIUS server but also busy RADIUS client machines.

Table 6-6, which can also be found on the FreeRADIUS web site (*http://www.freeradius.org*), lists the types of terminal servers supported, the method by which FreeRADIUS can communicate with them, what software module support it needs, and whether it requires an entry in the */etc/raddb/naspasswd* file.

Table 6-6. NAS compatibility with checkrad.pl

Vendor	Naslist type	Checkrad method	Modules required	Naspasswd entry required?
Lucent	ascend	SNMP	SNMP/BER	No
Nortel	Bay	Finger	Finger command	No
Cisco	Cisco	SNMP	SNMP/BER	Username: SNMP; Password: community
Computone	Computone	Finger	Finger command	No
Nortel	Cvx	SNMP	SNMP/BER	No
Digitro	Digitro	Rusers	Rusers command	No
Livingston	livingston	SNMP	SNMP/BER, ComOS 3.5 or later with SNMP	No
Lucent	Max40xx	finger	Finger command	No
VersaNet	versanet	SNMP	SNMP/BER	No
Various	portslave	finger	Finger command	No
Patton	patton	SNMP	SNMP/BER	No
Cyclades	pathras	telnet	Net::Telnet	Yes
Cyclades	Pr3000	SNMP	Snmpwalk command	No
Cyclades	Pr4000	SNMP	Snmpwalk command	No
USR/3Com	tc	telnet	Net::Telnet	Yes
USR/3Com	usrhyper	SNMP	SNMP/BER	No
USR/3Com	netserver	telnet	Net::Telnet	Yes

When It Goes Pear Shaped

When your simultaneous use enforcement doesn't seem to work right, try the following troubleshooting steps:

1. Make sure the NAS machine is contained in the *naslist* file and that its type is identified correctly.
2. Check the *naspasswd* file and make sure all is well.

3. Use the `-sx` flag when starting FreeRADIUS and look at the output to determine if it is seeing the `Simultaneous-Use` line.
4. Run *radcheck.pl* manually and see if it executes. This eliminates Perl version problems and module presence failures.

There are also some equipment-specific bugs that may be interfering with the functionality.

3Com and US Robotics equipment

3Com/US Robotics equipment has a tendency to incorrectly calculate SNMP object ID values. There is a workaround for this, however. First, make sure the HiPerArc software is updated to at least Version 4.2.32. To prevent simultaneous logins, you need to issue the following command on the NAS machine:

```
set pbus reported_port_density 256
```

Also, look at the *checkrad* program on the RADIUS server and comment out the following line, found under the subroutine *sub_usrhiper*:

```
($login) = /^.*\"([^"]+)".*$/;
```

Ascend equipment

You may see the following error entry in your log files:

```
Wed Jun 19 15:41:04 2002: Error: Check-TS: timeout waiting for checkrad
```

This problem usually occurs with MAX 4048 machines. To correct this, make sure that the NAS is correctly set up as a max40xx in the *naslist* file and double-check that Finger is enabled on the NAS machine. It can be found by going to the *Ethernet* menu, selecting *Mod Config* and setting *Finger* to *Yes*.

Cisco equipment

You may see the following error entry in your log files:

```
Wed Jun 19 17:09:16 2002: Error: Check-TS: timeout waiting for checkrad
```

This problem is mainly caused by not having SNMP enabled on the Cisco machine. Make sure the following line is present in the configuration file:

```
snmp-server community public RO 33
```

Replace *33* with the access list that distinguishes machines that can access SNMP information from those that can't. For example, the following access list does this:

```
access-list 33 permit 192.168.0.1
```

That line allows the machine at `192.168.0.1` to access the community information.

Monitoring FreeRADIUS

Part of proactive system administration is monitoring for problems before they occur. While you, as the administrator, are probably at your office and within reach of the RADIUS server for 8–12 hours a day, the remaining hours aren't devoid of users who depend on your service. What happens when (not if) your FreeRADIUS server has a problem and you're not around?

This section describes using some freely available tools to set up FreeRADIUS such that if it happens to shut down because of an error, it automatically restarts. While it's still your responsibility to troubleshoot the problem, it does recover the service so you don't have to deal with angry users calling because they can't get on the Internet.

Let's use Dan Bernstein's DaemonTools package, and in particular, its "supervise" service to monitor *radiusd*. To get started, surf to the DaemonTools web site at *http:// cr.yp.to/daemontools.html*, download the package, and install it. Dan has complete installation instructions on his site as well as a good deal more documentation that outlines and details the capabilities of DaemonTools. That's beyond the scope of this application, but it's likely you can find a use for some of the service management that DaemonTools provides.

Once the tools are installed, you need to create a RADIUS service directory that DaemonTools can use. It's common practice to place this directory on the */var* partition in the *svc* directory, although it can be placed anywhere you choose. For the rest of this section, I'll assume you chose the */var/svc/radiusd* directory. Make the directories, and then open up your favorite text editor.

In the text editor, you need to create a simple shell script, called *run*, that will call up *radiusd* in the event it fails. Here's a sample:

```
#!/bin/sh
exec /usr/local/sbin/radiusd -s -f
```

Of course, replace these directories with ones appropriate for your machine as needed. The -f flag is important in this case; it tells FreeRADIUS to stay on the console screen and not return to a command prompt. If it detaches itself, DaemonTools will think it died and attempt to restart it using the shell script provided above.

Now, make that script executable:

```
chmod +x /var/svc/radiusd/run
```

Finally, tell DaemonTools to watch FreeRADIUS.

```
Supervise /var/svc/radiusd.
```

DaemonTools is now setup and will restart *radiusd* upon its death.

Table 6-7 lists additional maintenance commands, available from the DaemonTools *svc* utility, that you will likely find useful.

Table 6-7. FreeRADIUS service management commands

Action	Command
To shut down FreeRADIUS normally	`svc -d /var/svc/radiusd`
To restart FreeRADIUS	`svc -u /var/svc/radiusd`
To kill FreeRADIUS (send a HUP)	`svc -h /var/svc/radiusd`
To shut down and stop monitoring	`svc -dx /var/svc/radiusd`

CHAPTER 7

Other RADIUS Applications

The previous two chapters have focused on using the FreeRADIUS product as the basis of an authentication/authorization/accounting system for a regular Internet service provider-style setup. In this chapter, I'll cover FreeRADIUS in conjunction with Web, LDAP, and email servers, and will discuss a utility, RadiusReport, for parsing RADIUS accounting files to glean valuable information from them.

RADIUS for Web Authentication

Chances are good that you have an area of your web site that needs to be protected from general public access. If you use the Apache web server, you may be familiar with the various methods by which this can be done: using an *.htaccess* and *.htpasswd* combination, setting Unix file system permissions, using Allow and Deny directives inside the Apache configuration file, and others. However, it's now possible to instruct Apache to authenticate against an existing RADIUS database of users, thereby protecting the area of your web site from unknown users and allowing access to those you trust.

This authentication is done using a module developed for Apache 1.x called *mod_auth_radius*. (Apache 2.0 had not been released at the time, and the module has yet to be updated for Version 2.0.) In effect, Apache becomes a RADIUS client—occupying the traditional position of the NAS in the authentication chain—and hits off the RADIUS server for authentication and accounting requests. Not only does this save administrative time by consolidating what potentially could become two user databases into one, but it also allows for more flexibility. Namely, RADIUS accounting can be used to track usage statistics for this protected site. Apache can keep detailed logs, but sometimes it's helpful to have all audit information in one place.

There are several potential applications for this module. The following scenarios are likely candidates for this module:

- A corporation who wants to create a special Intranet site specifically for its remote, mobile, and home users

- An Internet service provider who wishes to create a private site for subscribers only; perhaps a billing or support site that contains technical information suitable only for paying customers

- A web-based business that sells subscriptions to an online database or an online journal

And there are many others.

The Functionality

The *mod_radius_auth* module follows a predictable pattern in its use. A typical transaction occurs like this:

1. The browser submits a page request for *http://www.website.com/index.html*.

2. Apache sees that the directory is secured and sends an *Authorization Required* prompt (with spaces for the username and password) to the end user.

3. The user responds to the authentication request with his credentials. The browser sends the response, and the same page request once again, to Apache.

4. Apache receives the user's response and hands it off to *mod_auth_radius*. The module sees that a cookie is not present (since this is the user's first request.) It constructs a RADIUS request and transmits it to the RADIUS server.

5. The RADIUS server performs the authentication and sends its response back to *mod_auth_radius*.

6. *mod_auth_radius* interprets the RADIUS server's decision. If the authentication was deemed successful, the module sends a cookie with the public and private information hidden using MD5. If the authentication was unsuccessful, the module returns an *Access Denied* message.

7. The web browser sends the cookie with any other request. As long as *mod_auth_ radius* recognizes the cookie as valid, it will not send another request to the RADIUS server.

The cookies that are set on the end user's computer are valid for the lesser of the two values specified in the module's configuration and the secured area's configuration. The cookies also are killed when the browser ends, either by crash or via a user-initiated exit. The module will attempt to make cookies expire that, in its opinion, are too mature. However, if the browser does not acknowledge or follow through with the cookie expiration requests, the authentication prompt will appear repeatedly until the user reloads the browser and the site.

Configuring the Module

First, compile the module into Apache or use the *apxs* utility to instruct Apache to use *mod_auth_radius* as a dynamic module. You can obtain the module from its home page at *http://www.freeradius.org/mod_auth_radius*.

To compile the module statically into Apache itself, issue the following command:

```
./configure --add-module=/path/to/mod_auth_radius.c && make
```

The module is completely installed when the make process finishes without errors. Alternatively, to use *mod_auth_radius* as a dynamic module, use *apxs* as in the following example:

```
apxs -i -a -c mod_auth_radius.c
```

Next, edit the Apache *httpd.conf* file to instruct Apache to load the module. Include a line in the *LoadModule* section like this:

```
LoadModule radius_auth_module   libexec/mod_auth_radius.so
```

Then, scroll down to the *AddModule* section. Immediately following the line adding *mod_auth.c*, add the RADIUS module, as shown here:

```
AddModule mod_auth_radius.c
```

Now you need to create a section with specific configuration directives for the *mod_auth_radius* module. At the end of *httpd.conf*, create a section like the following example and configure it as explained next:

```
<IfModule mod_auth_radius.c>

AddRadiusAuth radiusservername:port sharedsecret timeout
AuthRadiusBindAddress 192.168.0.1
AddRadiusCookieValid 5

</IfModule>
```

The *AddRadiusAuth* directive tells Apache to authenticate against RADIUS. You specify the name of the RADIUS server, the port to use, the shared secret for the web client, and the timeout period Apache should wait before giving up and assuming no response will be sent. The *AuthRadiusBindAddress* directive specifies the *local* interface on which requests should be sent. The RADIUS server can then be set to accept requests only from this address for added security. (This directive is not required, since by default the module lets the underlying operating system choose the interface to use.) The *AddRadiusCookieValid* directive specifies the minutes for which the cookie sent in the response to the end user from the web client is valid. Setting this value to zero (0) signifies that the cookie will be valid forever.

The initial configuration is now complete. The next step is to define the areas of the web site that need protection. There are two ways to do this: (a) you can use an *.htaccess* file placed in the directory to be protected, or (b) you can define the locations inside *httpd.conf*. In this example, I'll assume that you've decided to define the locations inside *httpd.conf*. If you choose to use an *.htaccess* file, the directives between the <Location /secured/> and </Location> tags should be placed into the *.htaccess* file and subsequently saved into the directory to be secured.

To control access on a per-directory basis using *httpd.conf*, add the section to the file and configure it as such:

```
<Location /secured/>

AuthType Basic
AuthName "RADIUS authentication for localhost"
AuthAuthoritative off
AuthRadiusAuthoritative on
AuthRadiusCookieValid 5
AuthRadiusActive On
require valid-user

</Location>
```

The following definitions provide an explanation of each of these directives.

AuthType

This module requires basic authentication since digest authentication won't work correctly. (See Ben Laurie's *Apache: The Definitive Guide*, (O'Reilly), for more information on the two types.)

AuthName

The contents of this string are included in the password prompt presented to the end user. It simply serves to inform the user of which protected area he's attempting to enter.

AuthAuthoritative

This directive ensures that other authentication types are not used for this particular site area. You can net the same effect by commenting out other authentication types appearing previously in *httpd.conf*, but that is only recommended if this server is used only for this protected site.

AuthRadiusAuthoritative

This tells Apache to consider all RADIUS responses authoritative—that is, the RADIUS responses are "the final answer" (thanks, Regis).

AuthRadiusCookieValid

This is the same directive as the cookie setting globally set in the module configuration section. The server will choose the lower of the two values and set the cookie to expire at that interval. This value is in minutes.

AuthRadiusActive

This turns on RADIUS authentication globally. If there's an area of the site for which you want to use some other authentication method than RADIUS, set this directive to Off for that particular section. The default, if this directive is not included, is On.

Require valid-user
> This directive ensures that only valid users can access the site. If the RADIUS server returns anything but a valid user, access will not be permitted.

Using Challenge-Response with mod_auth_radius

The *mod_auth_radius* module is completely compliant with the challenge-response authentication method. However, end-user browser support is relatively limited: Netscape 3.x and 4.x and others support it well, but unfortunately, the browser with the largest hunk of market share, Internet Explorer, doesn't properly follow the RFC and, therefore, doesn't function correctly with challenge-response. You should certainly consider this caveat in determining whether to use challenge-response.

For supported browsers, the key to challenge-response is that the RADIUS cookies are set upon any authentication attempt. You can enter gibberish for your password and try to authenticate into a secured area, but while you are denied access because the password was incorrect, the cookie is being set with the RADIUS state attribute. The module also modifies Basic-Authentication-Realm. You then receive another prompt to try again, typically with a challenge. Once you enter the correct password (or the correct response to the challenge), all is well.

Limitations of the Module

Of course, opening any sort of private system to the Web presents a smorgasbord of security concerns. While Chapter 8 serves to detail the inherent problems and limitations of the RADIUS protocol, these limitations are still present using *mod_auth_radius* and should be considered.

First, using static passwords over the Web is not secure. The password from the end user to the web server is sent in plain text ("in the clear," that is) and is open to sniffing by anyone with the proper tools. This problem is exacerbated when the RADIUS server exists on the same machine as the web server. RADIUS was not designed to be directly exposed, and with script kiddies and crackers roaming about, it's a problem you simply don't want to have.

Second, using the same server for Web and dial-up users isn't the best idea, either. The problem lies in this: if the cracker manages to gain access to your web site using a sniffed password, he would have no trouble actually dialing up and gaining access to your system. He can pose as anyone and this becomes a serious threat to the integrity of your network. You might say that this seems almost a direct opposite to the benefits I was preaching about previously.

However, there are ways to work around these limitations:

- Use secure sockets layer (SSL) to protect the password.

- If you must open the web server to the Internet, protect the site with a secure server certificate (https) and purchase an SSL certificate from one of the many providers. This at least provides some protection for the passwords.

- Use one-time password (OTP) authentication. If you don't have the computing resources to separate the web server you want to protect and the RADIUS server, OTP significantly reduces the risk of password sniffing. See Chapter 8 for more information.

- Use your network architecture to your advantage. If your clients are dialing into a local area network—if they receive a private-class IP address such as 10.0.0.1, 172.16.0.1, or 192.168.0.1, for example—then the risk of snooping and sniffing is also moot. The *mod_auth_radius* module could then be used to protect user-specific information on the local network without opening the RADIUS passwords up to the entire Internet.

If you do decide to use OTP authentication, there are some caveats to the functionality of the module. When you access a site without stipulating a specific page on the site—*http://www.jonathanhassell.com/*, for example—Apache searches for files named *home.cgi*, *home.html*, *index.cgi*, and *index.html*. When *mod_radius_auth* looks for these files and it can't find them, it returns a 404 (Not Found) error. However, when it does find a file, it sets a cookie and returns a successful page request. The browser, though, might not use that cookie when it accesses another page on the site, which causes another authentication transaction with the RADIUS server (since the credentials include an OTP).

To work around this, surf to a page on the web site. Have that page contain a link to a specific location on the web site (i.e., *http://www.jonathanhassell.com/private/index. html*) and instruct the user to use that link to get to the secured area. This way, the user only has to use one authentication attempt to get to the secured pages. Note that this is only a real problem for implementations that use OTPs, but if static passwords are in use, multiple authentication attempts will take place. The credentials, however, are re-sent, and the user is not prompted: the only problem is the increased traffic, which may not be a significant limitation for your system.

Using the LDAP Directory Service

The ever-present complaint of systems administrators who deal with multiple user databases across multiple platforms is that of efficiency. Why can't all of my users be listed, configured, and managed from one set of tools? Why can't my various application servers—secured Web, email, newsgroups, and others—all tie into that one database and use its list? Without a centralized repository for user information, the effort of simply changing a password is multiplied by the number of systems on which a unique copy of the password is stored.

Fortunately, there is an answer, and better yet, it's standards based. The Lightweight Directory Access Protocol, or LDAP, is a directory-based database of information about users of a particular network. LDAP is a protocol that uses standard queries, much like SQL, to talk with a compliant backend. Using LDAP allows applications that support it to communicate with a centralized database and use its information in their internal operations. While a discussion about LDAP could fill volumes (and, in fact, has), the important fact to take away from this commentary is that FreeRADIUS has full and complete support for LDAP. This is part one of the equation. I have an LDAP client, but it needs something to talk to.

Enter CommuniGate Pro, an excellent email server product from the fine folks at Europe-based Stalker Software (*http://www.stalker.com*). CommuniGate Pro is designed to run on any number of processor architectures: from the Intel x86 regime to IBM's midrange servers and OS/400 computers. The product excels in every respect: it's intelligently designed, easy to install and use, and an excellent performer. The product has been subjected to numerous benchmarks in competition with other Internet mail servers and won each test hands down. It also is a fine LDAP server and can be configured to allow other applications to query its user database in full LDAP compliance. That's part two of our equation.

How does all of this fit together? Most organizations need email functionality. Of course, you're reading this book likely because your organization provides dial-up access to end users, either for profit or as part of your regular corporate business activities. Allowing FreeRADIUS, a robust RADIUS server, and CommuniGate Pro, an excellent mail server, to communicate with each other brings you the best of both worlds: stable server platforms and interoperability to ease the headaches of administration.

In this section, I'll detail how to make FreeRADIUS authenticate against the CommuniGate Pro LDAP user database. Most of the instructions in this section can be applied to any other LDAP database product, but there are a few instructions specific to CommuniGate Pro that are detailed. You can realize the benefits of this integration with any LDAP backend, but using CommuniGate Pro gives you a powerful email server to boot. On that note, let's begin!

Configuring FreeRADIUS to Use LDAP

To instruct FreeRADIUS to use the LDAP protocol instead of PAM or another local user authentication database, you need to install the OpenLDAP product. As of this writing, the latest version of OpenLDAP is 2.0.23. To install OpenLDAP on your system, perform the following steps:

1. Download the product, preferably in *.tar.gz* form, from the OpenLDAP web site at *http://www.openldap.org/software/download/*.

2. Decompress the program with the following command:

```
tar xzf openldap-stable-20010524.tar.gz
```

3. Change to the directory where the uncompressed files are and configure the program by executing the following:

```
cd openldap-2.0.11
./configure -sysconfdir=/etc --enable-slapd=no -enable-slurpd=no --with-
threads=no
```

4. Make the program's binaries with the following commands:

```
make depend
make
make install
cd ..
```

FreeRADIUS Versions

By press time, FreeRADIUS Version 0.6 should be released and available from the FreeRADIUS web site. However, the previous version, 0.5, has a buggy LDAP module that cannot handle transactions with LDAP servers that close their connections, such as CommuniGate Pro. The bug has been fixed in the development CVS system; however, the released versions have not been updated. If Version 0.6 is not available, a modified Version 0.5 with the repaired LDAP module code can be downloaded from the author's web site at *http://www.jonathanhassell.com*.

Now install FreeRADIUS with Version 0.6 or later. The latest information and updates to the FreeRADIUS product, as mentioned in Chapter 5, can be found at the official program web site at *http://www.freeradius.org*.

1. Download FreeRADIUS 0.6 or later.

2. Ensure that your Perl binaries are in your system path. If not, make a symbolic link from */usr/bin/perl* to their real location with a command similar to the following:

```
ln -s /usr/bin/perl /bin/perl
```

3. Decompress the program with the following command:

```
tar xzf freeradius-0.6-tar.gz
```

4. Change to the directory where the uncompressed files are and configure the program by executing the following:

```
cd freeradius-0.6
./configure -prefix=/usr --localstatedir=/var --sysconfdir=/etc --with-ldap --
without-rlm_x99_token
```

Note that the -without-rlm_x99_token directive is only needed for Red Hat Linux Versions 7.0 and earlier. Later versions do not require it.

5. Make the program's binaries with the following commands:

```
make
make install
```

Once the programs are installed, some edits to the FreeRADIUS configuration files are required. Inside the main configuration file, *radiusd.conf*, you must add a modules section that instructs FreeRADIUS to look for and use an LDAP connection. In this case, the LDAP server I want to specify is the CommuniGate Pro server. The following is an example configuration:

```
modules {
    ldap {
            server = "YourCommuniGateProServer.isp.com"
            port = 10389
            basedn = "cn=isp.com"
            filter = "(|(uid=%u)(uid=%U))"
            start_tls = no
            ldap_connections_number = 5
            timeout = 4
            timelimit = 3
            net_timeout = 1
            }
}
```

Next, add the LDAP protocol to the authenticate and authorize sections of *radiusd. conf*. Note that these protocols are followed in the order listed when FreeRADIUS is authenticating a user, so it's certainly possible and, in fact, good practice to set up alternate methods of authentication, both in anticipation of future needs and as a backup source of authentication. The following example shows this section of *radiusd.conf* configured appropriately to use LDAP and a MySQL database as well:

```
authorize {
    preprocess
    suffix
    files
    sql
    ldap
}
authenticate {
    ldap
}
preacct {
    suffix
    files
    preprocess
}
```

```
accounting {
    sql
    unix
    radutmp
}
```

Now that FreeRADIUS knows to use the LDAP module as a first point of authentication, that's all that is required on that end. Next, configure CommuniGate Pro to expect and listen for FreeRADIUS' communication.

Configuring CommuniGate Pro for LDAP Use

The CommuniGate Pro LDAP module is amazingly easy to configure. The only caveat with authenticating is that the CommuniGate Pro passwords have to be stored in plain text. However, you can configure the LDAP module in CommuniGate Pro to hide all passwords from all users—even the administrative-like postmaster user—so that they're not accessible from the outside.

First, CommuniGate Pro needs to know that the passwords for the users it knows about (in this case, the users with active email addresses) should be stored in the LDAP directory and not internally. From the administrative web interface, commonly on port 8010, navigate to the Domains menu and then select *Directory Integration*. Under the section called *Custom Account Settings*, select the option *Store Passwords in Regular Account Records*. Click the Update button to refresh the settings.

Next, tell the product to populate the LDAP database with the contents of its current internal database. Navigate to *Accounts* and then select *Domain Settings*. On that page, find the *Directory Integration* section and select *Keep in Sync*. Finally, click Delete All to flush the database, and then click Insert All to repopulate.

And that completes the configuration. You can test your setup using the NTRadPing utility or the *radtest* program, both of which are programs covered in Chapter 5.

Parsing RADIUS Accounting Files

One of the most useful aspects of RADIUS is the utility of its accounting portion. Logs from the RADIUS accounting server can be used for a multitude of purposes, including billing, usage planning, attack forensics, and auditing. Most Internet service providers have billing systems that directly import, analyze, interpret, and report the data contained within the accounting logs. But for corporate situations in which billing isn't required or for ISPs wanting information not provided by the billing system, it's useful to have a utility that will read the logs and report basic information for the outside of your standard reporting system.

Paul Gregg has created an excellent utility, written in Perl, called RadiusReport that offers this functionality. *RadiusReport* allows you to import log files and create different reports based on their contents. The utility supports the log files that FreeRADIUS generates, and it also has support for the following RADIUS servers:

- Livingston Radius, Versions 1.16, 2.0, and 2.01
- Dale Reed's RadiusNT
- Merit Radius
- Ascend Radius
- Radiator
- Novell's BorderManager Authentication Services (requires a separate utility to "massage" the format of the logs)

RadiusReport will generate all sorts of useful reports, including the projected telephone bill, reporting filtering based on specific months if you have multiple periods aggregated into a single file and parsing based on interim months. The reports are configured and constructed from command-line flags issued with the program call. The program will even read a compressed file, in case you use *gzip* or *tar* to compress and archive your old accounting logs.

RadiusReport is a Perl program, so it requires Version 5 of the language to be installed on the system. It also requires the POSIX module, which comes bundled with the Perl language in most cases. The utility needs POSIX compliance to correctly translate record date information into a timestamp field if your server doesn't make a timestamp.

RadiusReport can be downloaded from Paul Gregg's web site at *http://www.pgregg.com/projects/radiusreport/*.

Generating Reports

This section details the command-line flags necessary to instruct RadiusReport to generate specific types of reports. Table 7-1 lists the various parameters that can be issued to the program at runtime.

Table 7-1. RadiusReport command-line parameters

Parameter	Function
-f	Designates the raw log file from which to create the report
-h	Creates report without header and footer text
-I	Generates a report on IP addresses
-l	Specifies a user; use all for all users
-o	Creates individual report files for each user

Table 7-1. RadiusReport command-line parameters (continued)

Parameter	Function
-r	Generates a report on the most recent login times
-tba	Generates a full, detailed report
-tbac	Generates a full, detailed report with telephone company cost analysis

Example reports

The following command produces a minimal report for a specific user:

```
radiusreport -l rneis -f /var/adm/radacct/ptmstr-clt-1/detail
```

The resulting report looks similar to this:

```
Radius Log Report for: rneis
Date      Login    Logout   Ontime  Port
-------------------------------------------------------------------------
28/05/02 18:07:01 19:22:14  15m13s  A3
29/05/02 10:36:18 11:26:37  50m19s  A7
```

Issue the following command to produce a full report for a specific user:

```
radiusreport -tba -l rneis -f /var/adm/radacct/ptmstr-clt-1/detail
```

The result:

```
Radius Log Report for: rneis
Date      Login    Logout   Ontime   Port BW-In/Out       Total
-------------------------------------------------------------------------
28/05/02 13:18:19 13:38:07  19m48s  A5   120.1K/309.3K   0h19m
28/05/02 22:32:24 23:32:17  59m54s  A2   218.1K/1.7M     1h19m
29/05/02 19:54:33 21:15:01  80m29s  A3   396.7K/1.3M     2h40m
29/05/02 19:33:53 20:05:25  31m32s  A3   116.0K/1017.6K  54h24m
29/05/02 22:29:00 01:56:13  207m08s A1   1.2M/5.7M       57h51m
29/05/02 23:33:13 00:40:42  67m30s  A2   276.7K/1.0M     58h59m
-------------------------------------------------------------------------
  Total Hours:  58h59m
  Average Online times:   1h52m per day,   13h08m per week
  Total Data transferred In/Out: 18.2M/67.8M
```

The "Port" designation in these reports is the actual port number and an identifier—either A or I—to indicate whether the connection was asynchronous or based over ISDN. Also, the bandwidth statistics are generated based on the RADIUS client machine's transfer amounts and not total outbound bandwidth used.

The following command produces reports for every user for all the dates up to two months previous to the current day (the command should be placed on a single line):

```
radiusreport -tba -l all -f /var/adm/radacct/ptmstr-clt-1/archives/2002\
     /05/detail:/var/adm/radacct/ptmstr-clt-1/archives/2002/04/detail
```

The generated report can also be placed inside individual files per user in a specific directory. To do this, make a directory for the output and use the above command with the extra flag -o, followed by the destination directory.

The next command produces a list of users who used IP address 206.229.254.120. It assumes the log file is in the current directory.

```
radiusreport -i 206.229.254.120 -f detail
```

To produce a list of users, along with their last login times, use this command (it also assumes the log file is in the current directory):

```
radiusreport -r -f detail:detail.lastmonth
```

This command produces a complete user-to-IP mapping list. The log file is in the current directory in this example as well.

```
radiusreport -i 0 -f detail
```

The report generated by this command is a telephone company cost analysis for the user *sholmes* for April, but includes May's logs as well to ensure coverage of a login on April 30 extending into May 1 or beyond:

```
radiusreport -tbac -l sholmes -f detail.april:detail.may -d Apr
```

Using RadiusSplit

Paul Gregg has also created a utility to make the processing of log files go a bit faster by pre-processing them and splitting logs up into per-user files. When this utility, called RadiusSplit, is used in conjunction with RadiusReport, it's not uncommon to have a speed boost on the order of a factor of 100+, simply because log files are smaller and have less data irrelevant to the report being generated. For example, if you're processing a report for all the logins for the user *mdunlap* in May, the traditional log file would have that data, but also data for all the other users. Radius-Report would have to go record-by-record to determine whether the data pertained to the target user or if it was for another user. By using RadiusSplit, the RadiusReport program can go immediately to the split logs for *mdunlap* and process his logs immediately, without the extraneous data.

The small, single-file Perl program can be downloaded from Paul Gregg's web site as well at *http://www.pgregg.com/projects/radiussplit/*. The program reads the accounting log file and places copies of the relevant log file entries into individual user files in the following path:

```
/path/to/logfiles/yyyy/mm/username
```

yyyy and mm are the date on which the utility was run.

To use the program, use a standard Linux/Unix file display command and pipe the output to RadiusSplit. For example, for a log file stored in */var/adm/radacct/ptmstr-clt-1/detail*, use the following command:

```
tail -f /var/adm/radacct/ptmstr-clt-1/detail | radiussplit
```

Then, run RadiusReport, ensuring you include the correct paths to the newly split log files. The process is described in detail earlier in this chapter.

## CHAPTER 8

The Security of RADIUS

It's a little ironic that I'm devoting a chapter (albeit shorter than the others) to the security shortcomings of the RADIUS protocol, but it's something that needs doing. Unfortunately, RADIUS—a protocol designed from the outset to provide security so that only authorized users can take advantage of resources offered to a large group of people—has security problems, and some are actually quite serious.

The most prominent security vulnerability is rooted in RADIUS's wide use. It enjoys support from a number of network equipment vendors and is found in nearly all Internet service providers and corporate dial-up implementations. This popularity, however, is a double-edged sword. Security vulnerabilities in the core RADIUS protocol leave thousands upon thousands of systems open to compromise. Further, major changes can't be made to the core protocol, because that would run the risk of breaking compatibility with those same thousands upon thousands of systems that run RADIUS.

In this chapter, I'll discuss these vulnerabilities, offer some workarounds that protect your systems better, and close with a commentary from a security analyst on why users of RADIUS should push for minor protocol changes.

Vulnerabilities

It has been discovered by many that RADIUS has some fundamental flaws that may allow an attacker to compromise the integrity of a transaction. Primarily, the User-Password protection mechanism is inherently quite insecure, employing encryption and cryptographic techniques improperly. The concept of a response authenticator inside the RADIUS packet is genuinely good, but the implementation of such in the protocol is poorly designed. The Access-Request packet is not authenticated—at least as per the protocol specification—by any machine party to the transaction. The randomness of a client's generation of request authenticators is not really random enough. And finally, the shared secret is a primitive method of securing RADIUS client-to-server transactions.

Now I'll look at each of these vulnerabilities in greater detail.

MD5 and the Shared Secret

The shared secret is vulnerable because of the weak MD5 hash that hides the response authenticator. A hacker could easily attack the shared secret by sniffing a valid Access-Request packet and its corresponding response. He can easily get the shared secret by pre-computing the MD5 calculation from the code, ID, length, request authenticator, and attributes portion of the packets and then resuming the hash for each guess he makes.

The Access-Request Packet

There is no verification or authentication of the RADIUS Access-Request packet, as per the RFC specification, by default. The RADIUS server will perform a check to ensure that the message originated from an IP address listed as one of its clients, but in this day and age, spoofed IP addresses are easy to find and use. This is a serious limitation of the RADIUS protocol design.

As of now, the only workable solution is to require the presence of the Message-Authenticator attribute in all Access-Request messages. Briefly, the Message-Authenticator is the MD5 hash of the entire Access-Request message, using the client's shared secret as the key. When a RADIUS server is configured to only accept Access-Request messages with a valid Message-Authenticator attribute present, it must silently discard those packets with invalid or missing attributes. More information on the Message-Authenticator attribute can be found in Chapter 9 or in the RFC 2869.

If your implementation somehow prevents the use of the Message-Authenticator attribute, at least consider using some sort of account-lockout feature, which disables authentications after a specified number of authentication attempts within a specified time.

The User-Password Cipher Scheme

The way in which the User-Password attribute is handled, on a very general basis, is known as a stream cipher. A *stream cipher* is an encryption method that works with continuous streams of input, which is usually a stream of plain-text bits rather than fixed blocks; its opposite is a *block cipher*, which is an encryption method that processes input in fixed blocks of input, which are typically 64- or 128-bits long. A stream cipher generates a *keystream*, and this is used in the encryption: when you combine this *keystream* with the plain-text input stream using the XOR operation, the contents of the stream are encrypted. The generation of the *keystream* can be independent of the plain text and *ciphertext*, yielding what is termed a synchronous stream cipher, or it can depend on the data and its encryption, in which case the stream cipher is said to be self-synchronizing.

In the User-Password scheme, the first 16 octets act as a synchronous stream cipher, since the plain text input is independent of the *keystream*. However, after the first 16 octets, the *keystream* integrates the previous plain-text input and now becomes self-synchronizing. While this may seem overtly technical, the security of this cipher is questionable: the RADIUS protocol specification doesn't make clear what the requirements are for this cipher. MD5 hashes are generally meant to be crypto-graphic hashes, not stream ciphers. There may be a security problem in this possible misuse. Even the RADIUS RFC 2865 acknowledges this problem:

> The User-Password hiding mechanism described in Section 5.2 has not been subjected to significant amounts of cryptanalysis in the published literature. Some in the IETF community are concerned that this method might not provide sufficient confidential-ity protection [15] to passwords transmitted using RADIUS. Users should evaluate their threat environment and consider whether additional security mechanisms should be employed.

Unfortunately, the only way (at least using an Internet standard) to further secure the attributes and message of a RADIUS packet is to use the IPsec protocol with the encapsulated security payload (ESP) extensions and an encryption algorithm such as the triple data encryption standard (3DES). RFC 3162 describes this process in more detail.

The User-Password Shared Secret

Since the User-Password attribute is protected by a stream cipher, as described ear-lier, it's certainly possible for attackers to obtain information on the shared secret if they can sniff network traffic and try to authenticate against a RADIUS server. For example, an attacker could attempt to authenticate using a password known to him. He then receives and captures an Access-Request packet and uses a hash on a combi-nation of the protected portion of the User-Password and the password he originally used. Once that computation is complete, he has the result of the MD5 (shared secret + request authenticator) operation. He already knows the request authentica-tor from his original request, so he can now use a brute-force attack on the shared secret and determine it offline.

The User-Password Attribute and Password Attacks

An attacker can get around any rate limits of authentication placed by the adminis-trator of the RADIUS server because of the use of the stream cipher to protect the User-Password attribute. Here's how it works: the hacker first tries to authenticate against a RADIUS server using a known good username and a known, but probably incorrect, password. She takes the resulting Access-Request packet and figures out the MD5 result of the request authenticator + shared secret combination, as described earlier. She can then use a brute-force password attack by switching out the passwords in the packet and using the same request authenticator and shared secret. This will only work, however, if the password is less than or equal to 16 characters, since the User-Password cipher becomes self-synchronizing at the 17th character by including previous *ciphertext* in the encryption.

Attacks Using the Request Authenticator

There are several possible methods of attack on using the request authenticator portion of a RADIUS packet. In reality, all security in RADIUS is based on these authenticator fields, as they serve as unique and random "identifiers" (not to be confused with the ID field of the packet) for each packet. However, the ultimate security depends on how randomly these authenticators are generated. Most of the inherent security collapses when random number generators are used with cycles that are too short or values that are repeated. In this section, I'll take a look at some of the more probable attacks a hacker could wage against your systems through the request authenticator.

Repeated request authenticators and the User-Password attribute

It is possible to generate a bank of request authenticators and corresponding User-Password attributes if a hacker can sniff traffic on the wire between a RADIUS client and RADIUS server during a transaction. He can then see if any repeated values are used for the request authenticator; if they are, he can remove the shared secret from the first 16 octets of the password. In doing this, he gets the first 16 octets of two completely unprotected passwords that are XORed together.

Now, the bottom line here is that the attacker has gotten the first 16 octets unprotected. Most passwords that users choose, unfortunately, aren't even this long; even if they were, the hacker at least has a firm basis for a later brute-force attack. The attacker can't get any information at all *only* if all users have random passwords of the same length, which is a policy that would likely be applied and enforced by a system administrator. For this attack, a hacker wants two different passwords of significantly different lengths. Since the lowest length password has more padding, once the hacker completes his XOR he will have non-overlapping characters of the longer password exposed with minimal effort on his part.

Another attack can occur if a hacker attempts authentication multiple times using known passwords and intercepts the associated Access-Request packets. From these packets, she can get the request authenticator and the User-Password attribute. She then XORs the known password with the captured User-Password attribute and from the result, she has a valid bank of both request-authenticator values and the MD5 (request authenticator + shared secret) values. If she continues to sniff the wire and observes an request authenticator value that matches the one in her library, she can obtain the first 16 octets of the User-Password by looking up the MD5 sum from her library and XORing it with the User-Password attribute. As well, using this library of request authenticators, the hacker could also add appropriate identifiers and server responses she obtained by sniffing the wire. She could then masquerade as the server and replay the old server responses when an appropriate Access-Request packet came through.

Shared secrets

The use of a shared secret in the RADIUS protocol is one of the worst design decisions possible within the context of network security. By default, the RADIUS protocol specification allows the same shared secret to be used among any number of clients. Because of this, from a hacker's point of view, all RADIUS clients that use the same shared secret can effectively be considered the same client for their purposes. If one client is flawed, that machine can be compromised and used to compromise other machines not inherently flawed, since the shared secret was exposed. Additionally, only ASCII characters, of which there are 94 in total, are allowed to be used in making up a shared secret. Even more stringently, the shared secret is usually limited to 16 characters or less. This makes it nearly infinitely easier for an attacker to guess the shared secret, since he has finite bounds for both the characters and the length of the secret that he is trying to guess.

The Extensible Authentication Protocol

EAP is an extension to the PPP protocol that enables a variety of authentication protocols to be used. EAP is not tightly bound to the security method. It passes through the exchange of authentication messages, allowing the authentication software stored in a server to interact with its counterpart in the client. EAP serves as a sort of replacement protocol, allowing the initial negotiation of an authentication protocol (such as CHAP and MS-CHAP Versions 1 and 2) and then the agreement on both ends of the connection on a link type, which is a specific EAP-authentication scheme. Once these two elements have been confirmed, EAP allows for an open-ended conversation between a RADIUS server and its client.

EAP is designed to function as an authentication "plug-in," with libraries on both the client and the server end of a PPP connection. Each authentication scheme is associated with a particular library file, and once a specific library has been dropped into place on both ends, that new scheme can be used. Thus, the protocol can easily be functionally extended by vendors at any time without having to redesign the whole protocol. EAP currently supports authentication schemes such as Generic Token Card, OTP, MD5-Challenge, and Transport Level Security (TLS) for use in smartcard applications and support for certificates. In addition to supporting PPP, EAP is also supported in the link layer as specified in IEEE 802. IEEE 802.1x defines EAP's use in authenticating 802 devices, like WiFi access points and Ethernet switches.

How does EAP relate to RADIUS? EAP secures RADIUS more. Using RADIUS with EAP is not an official authentication scheme of EAP; rather, look at it as the passing of EAP messages of any EAP type by the RADIUS client gear and the RADIUS server. EAP over RADIUS is typically set up in this fashion: the access server is configured to use EAP and also to use RADIUS as its authentication provider. When a service consumer attempts to connect, the service consumer negotiates the use of EAP with the RADIUS client gear. The end user then sends an EAP message to the RADIUS client, and the RADIUS client encapsulates the EAP message as a RADIUS message and sends it to the RADIUS server. The RADIUS server acts on the encapsulated message and sends a RADIUS-style message back to the RADIUS client. The RADIUS client then constructs an EAP message from the RADIUS message and sends it back to the service consumer/end user. Figure 8-1 illustrates this flow.

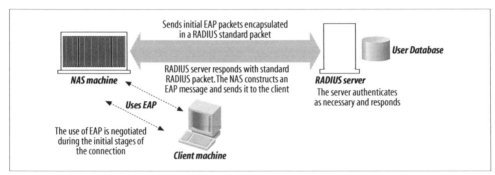

Figure 8-1. EAP and RADIUS working together

Compensating for the Deficiencies

All of the security issues presented in this chapter have workarounds. Some have been listed within the discussion of each vulnerability, but this section serves as a quick reference checklist, from which you can decide which workarounds to employ in your RADIUS implementation. This section outlines some of the basic steps you can use to compensate for some of the more nefarious RADIUS design decisions:

Use the IPsec protocol with ESP and an encryption algorithm such as 3DES.
  When IPsec encrypts the whole RADIUS message, fields open to compromise—namely the request authenticator fields and the User-Password, Tunnel-Password, and MPPE-Key attributes—cannot be viewed. To decrypt these fields, an attacker first must break into the ESP-protected message. This protects the entire RADIUS message and keeps it from prying eyes.

Require any shared secrets in use to be either 22 keyboard characters long or 32 hexadecimal digits long.
  This protects against the deficiencies and the unprotected nature of the shared secret concept.

Use a different shared secret for each RADIUS client and server pair.
This is just a basic security measure, much like having a different password for a variety of web sites and computing resources.

Use the Message-Authenticator *attribute in all* Access-Request *messages. On the client side, make sure the* Message-Authenticator *is used and ensure it can be configured.*
On the server side, require that the Message-Authenticator attribute be present and also allow here for its configuration. This compensates for having no Access-Request messages authenticated anywhere along the transaction path.

Use a cryptographic-quality random number generator to generate the request authenticator.
This offsets the rather limited quality of the request authenticator's implementation.

You might also consider protecting the links from the end user to the RADIUS client gear using EAP and one of the strong encryption types available with its use. For example, you could use EAP-TLS, which is a strong EAP method that requires the exchange of client and RADIUS server certificates. The use of EAP messages inherently requires a valid Message-Authenticator certificate, which protects messages that can't otherwise be protected by the use of IPsec.

Also, along with EAP, think about using mutual authentication methods. Very simply, both ends of the connection authenticate their peer in mutual authentication. The authentication attempt is rejected if either end's authentication fails. EAP-TLS is a mutual authentication method: the RADIUS server validates the user certificate of the client, and the client validates the computer certificate of the RADIUS server.

Finally, if the PAP authentication protocol is not required, disable it on both the client and the server end. PAP should only be used as a secure connection when it's used in conjunction with OTP and Token Card authentication where the password is reasonably complex and changes with each use. However, even in this situation, having PAP enabled allows for misconfigured end users to negotiate with the RADIUS client gear and at that point, they could potentially send unprotected passwords. If at all possible, use EAP with the OTP and Token Card authentication types instead of PAP. In the same line of thinking, disable LAN Manager encoding if you use MS-CHAP.

Modifying the RADIUS Protocol

It may be frustrating to have to employ workarounds to inherent deficiencies in the RADIUS protocol. As informed, knowledgeable RADIUS users (and you are knowledgeable now that you are reading this book), we need to push for a protocol revision. Joshua Hill, of InfoGard Laboratories, eloquently makes a case for a revision in the following mini-essay.

So, why attempt to modify RADIUS at all? Why not just go to another (presumably more modern and more secure) protocol? Well, for the most part, the answer is, "because such a protocol doesn't currently exist." In the near future, however, Diameter is likely to be released by the IETF.

Diameter is the planned RADIUS replacement. The great majority of all the protocol work that has gone into Diameter has been directed at removing some of the functional limitations imposed by the RADIUS protocol. Effectively, no work has been done that relates to the client/server security of the protocol. (CMS is defined, but this is a security layer for the proxy to proxy interaction, not the client to proxy/server interaction.)

So, does this mean that they continue to use even RADIUS' ad hoc system? No: they removed all security functionality from the protocol. In essence, the developers did the protocol designer's equivalent of punting. Section 2.2 of the current Diameter protocol spec says:

"Diameter clients, such as Network Access Servers (NASes) and Foreign Agents MUST support IP Security, and MAY support TLS. Diameter servers MUST support TLS, but the administrator MAY opt to configure IPSec instead of using TLS. Operating the Diameter protocol without any security mechanism is not recommended."

So, IPSec and/or TLS handle all security aspects of the protocol. From a security aspect, this strikes me as a very good idea. Both IPSec and TLS are fully featured (sometimes too fully featured) protocols that many people have reviewed. That's already much better than RADIUS ever did.

Examining this from a slightly different angle gives me some cause for concern, however. It strikes me that the overhead imposed by a full TLS/IPSec implementation is very significant for many current-day embedded devices. This would seem to indicate that (at least in the near future) manufactures are going to either continue to use RADIUS or ignore the Diameter standard and perform Diameter without TLS or IPSec.

Because of this, I suspect that it would be advantageous to push for at least minimal RADIUS protocol revision.

## CHAPTER 9

New RADIUS Developments

Up to this point, I've covered the contents and specifications of the original RADIUS RFC drafts. Since those drafts were approved and published, new advancements in technology have mandated some revisions to those RFCs, particularly in the areas of tunnel support and new security technologies. In this chapter, I'll cover these updates and how they might affect your current implementation or any changes you will make in the future.

Interim Accounting Updates

RADIUS now includes support for interim accounting updates. Prior to the issuing of the RADIUS Extensions RFC in June 2000, accounting updates were done primarily at the beginning and end of a transaction, when the server received Accounting-Start and Accounting-Stop packets from the user. However, now the server can include the Acct-Interim-Interval attribute in the message. The value of this attribute is the time (in seconds) between accounting update messages. An administrator can also choose to configure a minimum value locally on the RADIUS client, but this value always overrides any Acct-Interim-Interval value found in an Access-Accept packet.

This attribute can include all the attributes found in the standard Accounting Stop message except the Acct-Term-Cause attribute. The data sent within the Acct-Interim-Interval packet is always cumulative; that is to say, the data in each interim update contains data from the start of the session through the current state of the session at the time the packet is sent. Because this data is cumulative, it's up to the RADIUS client gear to ensure that only one interim update packet exists on the wire at once. Some RADIUS client machines may choose to add a delay of some amount of seconds to make sure that the previous condition is satisfied.

The Apple Remote Access Protocol

The Apple Remote Access Protocol (ARAP) sends traffic based on the AppleTalk protocol across PPP links and ISDN switched-circuit networks. ARAP is still pervasive in the Apple market, although the company is attempting to transition into an Apple-specific TCP stack for use over a PPP link. ARAP support is typically found in most RADIUS client gear, and RADIUS now supports authenticating based on the ARAP protocol.

ARAP authentication typically takes one to two steps, as follows:

1. The first step is basically a mutual authentication with an exchange of random numbers signed with a *key*, which happens to be the user's password. The RADIUS client challenges and authenticates the dial-in client, and the dial-in client challenges and authenticates the RADIUS client challenges. First, the RADIUS client sends random numbers of 32 bits to the dial-in client inside an ARAP msg_auth_challenge packet. Then, the dial-in client uses his password to encrypt the two random numbers sent by the RADIUS client with DES. The dial-in client sends the result back in a msg_auth_request packet. Finally, the RADIUS client unencrypts the message based on the password it has on record for the user and verifies the random numbers are intact. If so, it encrypts the challenge from the dial-in client and sends it back in a msg_auth_response packet.

2. The RADIUS client may initiate a second phase of authentication using optional *add-in security modules*, which are small pieces of code that are run on both ends of the connection and provide read and write access across the link. Some security token vendors use these add-ins to perform their own proprietary authentication.

There are some caveats to integrating ARAP and RADIUS based on the way ARAP is designed. Namely, ARAP transmits more security profile information after the first phase completes but before the second phase of authentication begins. The profile information is contained within a single attribute and is a series of numeric characters relating to passwords. Even so, challenge responses and this new profile information must exist at times that may seem a bit non-standard. But it *is* the standard.

To allow an ARAP-based client access to the resources the RADIUS server is protecting, an Access-Request packet must be issued on behalf of the ARAP client. This process takes place as one would imagine: the RADIUS client with the ARAP protocol generates a challenge based on a random number and, in response from the end-user client, receives the challenge and the username. The relevant data is then forwarded to the RADIUS server inside a standard RADIUS Access-Request packet. The data that is transplanted is as follows: User-Name, Framed-Protocol with a value of 3 for ARAP, ARAP-Password, and any other pertinent information like Service-Type, NAS-IP-Address, NAS-Id, NAS-Port-Type, NAS-Port, NAS-Port-Id, Connect-Info, and others. Note that only one of the User-Password, CHAP-Password, or ARAP-Password attributes needs to be present in the Access-Request packet. Any EAP-Messages attributes super-cede any of those attributes' presence in a packet.

The authentication then takes place. If the RADIUS server doesn't support ARAP, it should return an Access-Reject message. If it does, then in order to authenticate the user it should verify the user response using the challenge, found in the first eight octets of the request authenticator, and the associated response, found in the first eight octets of the ARAP-Password attribute. The resulting Access-Accept message, if this information is verified and the user is indeed successfully authenticated, should be formatted in the following manner:

- The ID and Response Authenticator fields should be included as per the normal RADIUS standard.
- The Service-Type attribute should be Framed-Protocol.
- The Framed-Protocol attribute should be set to a value of 3, signifying ARAP.
- The Session-Timeout attribute should be set to the maximum connect time. It can also be set for unlimited time by either setting the value to -1 or not including the attribute in the packet. All machines party to the transaction will consider the absence of attribute to mean the user is allowed unlimited connect time.
- The ARAP-Challenge-Response attribute should be set to a value of eight octets of the response to the challenge. The RADIUS server forms this by finding the challenge from the last eight octets of the ARAP-Password attributes and performing DES encryption using the password of the user as the key.
- The ARAP-Features attribute contains information that the RADIUS client should encapsulate in a feature flags packet in the ARAP protocol.
- A single Reply-Message of up to 253 text characters can be included.
- Framed-AppleTalk-Network may be included.
- Framed-AppleTalk-Zone, of up to 32 characters, may also be included.

Zones are an interesting concept that deserve some commentary. The ARAP protocol maps this concept of zones, which designate access privileges a user may have that correspond with an area or a set of resources. A Zone Access Flag is defined along with a list of configured zones; this access flag specifies how the user is allowed to access the zones in the list. For example, the user might be able to use only the default zone's resources, or he may be allowed to use only the zones in an accompanying list, or he may be allowed to see all zones *except* those in his list. The RADIUS client gear handles zones by using configured filters with the same names as the ARAP zones. It uses the ARAP-Zone-Access attribute, which contains an integer similar to the zone access flag. The name of the zone is then transplanted by the RADIUS client into pertinent RADIUS packets using the standard RADIUS Filter-ID attribute.

The Extensible Authentication Protocol

EAP is supported in the new RADIUS extensions and allows for new authentication types to be used over links running on the PPP protocol. Authentication schemes such as public key, smart cards, one-time passwords, Kerberos, and others are supported over PPP when EAP is used. To support EAP, RADIUS includes two new attributes—EAP-Message and Message-Authenticator—that are described in this section.

Typically, the RADIUS server acts as an intermediary between the client and a back-room proprietary security and authentication server. It normally encapsulates the EAP packets within a standard RADIUS packet, using the EAP-Message attribute, and then transmits them back and forth between the two machines. This lets the RADIUS server talk to the other proprietary authentication server using a standard protocol that requires no special modifications on the RADIUS server. It can still fully support standard RADIUS requests with reduced overhead.

A typical EAP over RADIUS transaction occurs in a standard format, which is outlined here:

1. The dial-up client and the RADIUS client gear negotiate the use of EAP within their specific link control protocol—this is most commonly PPP.
2. The RADIUS client then sends an EAP-Request/Identity message to the client unless its identity has been verified through some other means, such as callback or caller ID.
3. The dial-up client then responds with an EAP-Response/Identity message.
4. The RADIUS client gear receives this response from the client and forwards it to the RADIUS server inside a standard RADIUS Access-Request using the EAP-Message attribute.
5. The RADIUS server responds with a standard Access-Challenge packet that contains an EAP-Message attribute. The EAP-Message attribute contains a full EAP packet.
6. The RADIUS client gear unwraps the encapsulated EAP message and forwards it to the dial-up client.

The authentication continues as many times as needed until either an Access-Reject message or an Access-Accept message is received. If the EAP transaction follows these typical steps, then the RADIUS client gear will never have to manipulate an EAP packet. Of course, the world is not always as simple as that; as such, there are a couple of caveats to this scenario.

First, you must permit proxy capability between RADIUS machines that may not be compliant with the EAP protocol. If the RADIUS client machine sends the EAP-Request/Identity, as described previously in step two, the RADIUS client has to copy the relevant information into the appropriate fields in a standard RADIUS packet. For example, the contents of the EAP-Response/Identity packet need to be copied into the User-Name attribute. As well, the NAS-Port or NAS-Port-ID attributes should be included in the Access-Request packet, and the NAS-Identifier and NAS-IP-Address attributes *must* be included. (All of this must, of course, be present in the subsequent packets exchanged between the proxy machines and the original, EAP-compliant RADIUS server.) All of this is to facilitate accounting.

Second, the RADIUS client may not always issue the EAP-Request/Identity packet. Primarily, this occurs when the identity of a user has been verified through some other means, such as a callback and caller-ID value. You can tell this has happened when the Called-Station-ID or Calling-Station-ID attributes are present in a RADIUS packet (these are required to be present when identity is verified through their use). In this case, the RADIUS client sends a standard Access-Request packet to the RADIUS server with an EAP-Message; inside that message is the EAP-Start instruction, which is indicated by sending an EAP-Message attribute with a length of two octets. This method, although convenient, is not within the RADIUS specification as per RFC 2865, and there are problems with this approach when proxies are in use.

Examples of an EAP Conversation

Figure 9-1 is an example of a transaction between a dial-up client, a RADIUS client box, and an EAP-compliant RADIUS server using the OTP authentication scheme. (This is the same example used in the RADIUS Extensions RFC, number 2869. It has been remodeled for clarity and potentially better visual comprehension.)

Potential Uses

EAP has a lot of potential, although its current uses are limited since most of the protocols it uses to talk with a backend security authenticator are proprietary, largely due to a lack of standardization. However, RADIUS over EAP compensates for some of the security deficiencies of the core RADIUS protocol's design, as discussed at length in Chapter 8, and is recommended for use where appropriate.

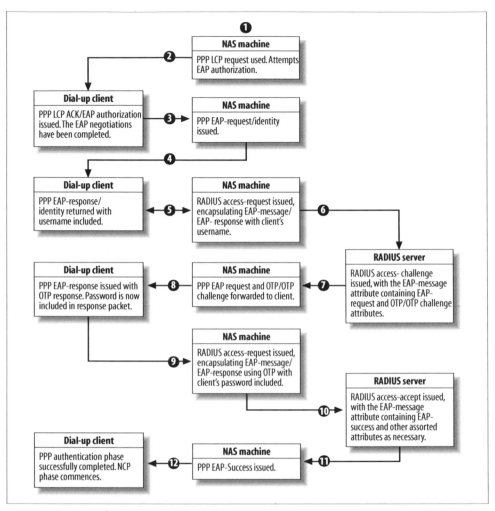

Figure 9-1. A typical RADIUS over EAP transaction

Tunneling Protocols

With the advent of work-from-home strategies and the branch-office concept becoming ever more popular, the dependence on access to corporate networks and privatized ISPs has become stronger. There exists a way to use a sort of tunnel to log in to corporate network over the Internet and access that network's resources as though you were locally attached to it. Although discussing tunnels is beyond the scope of this book, RADIUS does support a variety of tunneling protocols, both voluntary and compulsory. New RADIUS attributes were introduced with RFC 2868 that provide support for this emerging technology.

As well, private ISPs and even some corporate IT data centers want to be able to account for the use of their service for accounting, billing, and auditing purposes. RADIUS accounting, of course supporting the AAA model as discussed in Chapter 1, is an obvious way to collect this data, especially with the new tunneling-support attributes, some modifications to the Acct-Status-Type attribute, and some entirely new attributes specifically focused at RADIUS accounting.

The new values for the Acct-Status-Type attribute are listed in Table 9-1.

Table 9-1. New values per RFC 2867 for Acct-Status-Type

Value	Name	Description	Also requires
9	Tunnel-Start	Marks the creation of a tunnel with another end point.	User-Name, NAS-IP-Address, Acct-Delay-Time, Event-Timestamp, Tunnel-Type, Tunnel-Medium-Type, Tunnel-Client-Endpoint, Tunnel-Server-Endpoint, Acct-Tunnel-Connection
10	Tunnel-Stop	Marks the destruction of a tunnel with another node.	User-Name, NAS-IP-Address, Acct-Delay-Time, Acct-Input-Octets, Acct-Output-Octets, Acct-Session-ID, Acct-Session-Time, Acct-Input-Packets, Acct-Output-Packets, Acct-Terminate-Cause, Acct-Multi-Session-Id, Event-Timestamp, Tunnel-Type, Tunnel-Medium-Type, Tunnel-Client-Endpoint, Tunnel-Server-Endpoint, Acct-Tunnel-Connection, Acct-Tunnel-Packets-Lost
11	Tunnel-Reject	Marks the rejection of an attempt to establish a tunnel with another node.	User-Name, NAS-IP-Address, Acct-Delay-Time, Acct-Terminate-Cause, Event-Timestamp, Tunnel-Type, Tunnel-Medium-Type, Tunnel-Client-Endpoint, Tunnel-Server-Endpoint, Acct-Tunnel-Connection
12	Tunnel-Link-Start	Marks the creation of a tunnel link; for those protocols that support multiple links per tunnel.	User-Name, NAS-IP-Address, NAS-Port, Acct-Delay-Time, Event-Timestamp, Tunnel-Type, Tunnel-Medium-Type, Tunnel-Client-Endpoint, Tunnel-Server-Endpoint, Acct-Tunnel-Connection
13	Tunnel-Link-Stop	Marks the destruction of a tunnel link; for those protocols that support multiple links per tunnel.	User-Name, NAS-IP-Address, NAS-Port, Acct-Delay-Time, Acct-Input-Octets, Acct-Output-Octets, Acct-Session-Id, Acct-Session-Time, Acct-Input-Packets, Acct-Output-Packets, Acct-Terminate-Cause, Acct-Multi-Session-Id, Event-Timestamp, NAS-Port-Type, Tunnel-Type, Tunnel-Medium-Type, Tunnel-Client-Endpoint, Tunnel-Server-Endpoint, Acct-Tunnel-Connection, Acct-Tunnel-Packets-Lost
14	Tunnel-Link-Reject	Marks the rejection of an attempt to establish a tunnel link; for those protocols that support multiple links per tunnel.	User-Name, NAS-IP-Address, Acct-Delay-Time, Acct-Terminate-Cause, Event-Timestamp, Tunnel-Type, Tunnel-Medium-Type, Tunnel-Client-Endpoint, Tunnel-Server-Endpoint, Acct-Tunnel-Connection

The new tunnel-accounting attributes are integrated with the rest of the RADIUS extensions attributes in the next section.

New Extensions Attributes

In the familiar (yet repetitive, I know) format of Chapter 2, I will now detail the new attributes offered in RFC 2869, as well as those specified in the "RADIUS Attributes for Tunnel Protocol Support" (RFC 2868) and "RADIUS Accounting Modifications for Tunnel Protocol Support" (RFC 2867). They are presented in ascending order of the attribute number.

Acct-Input-Gigawords

Attribute Number	52
Length	6
Value	INTEGER
Allowed in	Accounting-Request
Prohibited in	Access-Accept, Access-Request, Access-Reject, Access-Challenge, Accounting-Response
Presence in Packet	Not required
Maximum Iterations	1

The value of this attribute is the number of times that the Acct-Input-Octets counter has exceeded and wrapped over 2^{32} since this transaction's inception. It can only be present in Accounting-Request packets where the value of the Acct-Status-Type is either *Stop* or *Interim-Update*.

Acct-Output-Gigawords

Attribute Number	53
Length	6
Value	INTEGER
Allowed in	Accounting-Request
Prohibited in	Access-Accept, Access-Request, Access-Reject, Access-Challenge, Accounting-Response
Presence in Packet	Not required
Maximum Iterations	1

The value of this attribute is the number of times that the Acct-Output-Octets counter has exceeded and wrapped over 2^{32} since this transaction's inception. It can only be present in Accounting-Request packets where the value of the Acct-Status-Type is either *Stop* or *Interim-Update*.

Event-Timestamp

Attribute Number	55
Length	6
Value	INTEGER

Allowed in	Accounting-Request
Prohibited in	Access-Accept, Access-Request, Access-Reject, Access-Challenge, Accounting-Response
Presence in Packet	Not required
Maximum Iterations	1

This attribute indicates the time at which an event marked by the transmission of an Accounting-Request packet occurred. The value is represented as an integer in the typical Unix-style time notation: the number of seconds since January 1, 1970 00:00 UTC.

Tunnel-Type

Attribute Number	64
Length	6
Value	ENUM
Allowed in	Access-Request, Accept-Accept, Accounting-Request
Prohibited in	Access-Reject, Access-Challenge, Accounting-Response
Presence in Packet	Not required
Maximum Iterations	1

This attribute is an enumerated value that indicates the tunneling protocol specified for a particular session. If the attribute is present in an Access-Request packet, the RADIUS server should read its presence as a hint; it is not required to honor that request.

The possible values for the Tunnel-Type attribute and their corresponding meanings are listed in Table 9-2.

Table 9-2. Tunnel-Type enumerated values

Value	Tunneling protocol
1	Point-to-Point Tunneling Protocol (PPTP)
2	Layer Two Forwarding (L2F)
3	Layer Two Tunneling Protocol (L2TP)
4	Ascend Tunnel Management Protocol (ATMP)
5	Virtual Tunneling Protocol (VTP)
6	IP Authentication Header in the Tunnel-mode (AH)
7	IP-in-IP Encapsulation (IP-IP)
8	Minimal IP-in-IP Encapsulation (MIN-IP-IP)
9	IP Encapsulating Security Payload in the Tunnel-mode (ESP)
10	Generic Route Encapsulation (GRE)
11	Bay Dial Virtual Services (DVS)
12	IP-in-IP Tunneling

Tunnel-Medium-Type

Attribute Number	65
Length	6
Value	ENUM
Allowed in	Access-Request, Accept-Accept
Prohibited in	Access-Reject, Access-Challenge, Accounting-Request, Accounting-Response
Presence in Packet	Not required
Maximum Iterations	1

This attribute is an enumerated value that indicates the transport medium to use when creating a tunnel based on a protocol that can support multiple tunnel types. If the attribute is present in an Access-Request packet, the RADIUS server should read its presence as a hint; it is not required to honor that request.

The possible values for the Tunnel-Medium-Type attribute and their corresponding meanings are listed in Table 9-3.

Table 9-3. Tunnel-Medium-Type enumerated values

Value	Tunnel Medium Types
1	IPv4 (IP Version 4)
2	IPv6 (IP Version 6)
3	NSAP
4	HDLC (8-bit multidrop)
5	BBN 1822
6	802 (includes all 802 media plus Ethernet "canonical format")
7	E.163 (POTS)
8	E.164 (SMDS, Frame Relay, ATM)
9	F.69 (Telex)
10	X.121 (X.25, Frame Relay)
11	IPX
12	AppleTalk
13	Decnet IV
14	Banyan Vines
15	E.164 with NSAP format subaddress

Tunnel-Client-Endpoint

Attribute Number	66
Length	3 or more octets
Value	STRING

Allowed in	Access-Request, Access-Accept, Accounting-Request
Prohibited in	Access-Reject, Access-Challenge, Accounting-Response
Presence in Packet	Not required
Maximum Iterations	1

The Tunnel-Client-Endpoint attribute contains the address of the initiator of the tunnel. It's designed to work in conjunction with the Tunnel-Server-Endpoint and Acct-Tunnel-Connection-ID attributes to provide a way to identify a specific tunnel for accounting, billing, and auditing functions. If the tunnel is an IPv4 tunnel, then the value of this attribute is either the FQDN of the initiator end of the tunnel or the dotted-decimal (*x.x.x.x*) address of the initiator. If the tunnel is an IPv6 tunnel, the string is either the FQDN as described here or a textual representation of the address. All other tunnel formats use a tag that refers to local configuration data specific to the medium.

Tunnel-Server-Endpoint

Attribute Number	67
Length	3 or more octets
Value	STRING
Allowed in	Access-Request, Access-Accept, Accounting-Request
Prohibited in	Access-Reject, Access-Challenge, Accounting-Response
Presence in Packet	Not required
Maximum Iterations	1

The Tunnel-Server-Endpoint attribute contains the address of the initiator of the tunnel. It's designed to work in conjunction with the Tunnel-Client-Endpoint and Acct-Tunnel-Connection-ID attributes to provide a way to identify a specific tunnel for accounting, billing, and auditing functions. If the tunnel is an IPv4 tunnel, then the value of this attribute is either the FQDN of the receiving (server) end of the tunnel or the dotted-decimal (*x.x.x.x*) address of the receiver. If the tunnel is an IPv6 tunnel, the string is either the FQDN as described here or a textual representation of the address. All other tunnel formats use a tag that refers to local configuration data specific to the medium.

Acct-Tunnel-Connection

Attribute Number	68
Length	3 or more octets
Value	STRING
Allowed in	Accounting-Request
Prohibited in	Access-Accept, Access-Request, Access-Reject, Access-Challenge, Accounting-Response
Presence in Packet	Not required
Maximum Iterations	1

This attribute defines the identifier assigned to a specific tunnel session. This attribute works in conjunction with Tunnel-Client-Endpoint and Tunnel-Server-Endpoint to uniquely identify a specific session for accounting, auditing, and billing purposes. The field encoding for the value of this attribute is implementation specific.

Tunnel-Password

Attribute Number	69
Length	5 or more octets
Value	STRING
Allowed in	Access-Accept
Prohibited in	Access-Request, Access-Reject, Access-Challenge, Accounting-Response, Accounting-Request
Presence in Packet	Not required
Maximum Iterations	1

This attribute contains the password for authenticating to a remote server and includes a "salt" field that is used to verify the uniqueness of the key used to encrypt the tunnel password.You can find more information at the RFC 2868, but no sense sending you off on a chase. Here's the relevant part:

> The plaintext String field consists of three logical sub-fields: the Data-Length and Password sub-fields (both of which are required), and the optional Padding sub-field. The Data-Length sub-field is one octet in length and contains the length of the unencrypted Password sub-field. The Password sub-field contains the actual tunnel password. If the combined length (in octets) of the unencrypted Data-Length and Password sub-fields is not an even multiple of 16, then the Padding sub-field MUST be present. If it is present, the length of the Padding sub-field is variable, between 1 and 15 octets. The String field MUST be encrypted as follows, prior to transmission:

> Construct a plaintext version of the String field by concatenating the Data-Length and Password sub-fields. If necessary, pad the resulting string until its length (in octets) is an even multiple of 16. It is recommended that zero octets (0x00) be used for padding. Call this plaintext P. Call the shared secret S, the pseudo-random 128-bit Request Authenticator (from the corresponding Access-Request packet) R, and the contents of the Salt field A. Break P into 16 octet chunks $p(1), p(2)...p(i)$, where $i = len(P)/16$. Call the *ciphertext* blocks $c(1), c(2)...c(i)$ and the final *ciphertext* C. Intermediate values $b(1), b(2)...c(i)$ are required. Encryption is performed in the following manner (+ indicates concatenation):

> ```
> b(1) = MD5(S + R + A)    c(1) = p(1) xor b(1)  C = c(1)
> b(2) = MD5(S + c(1))     c(2) = p(2) xor b(2)  C = C + c(2)
> b(i) = MD5(S + c(i-1))   c(i) = p(i) xor b(i)  C = C + c(i)
> ```

> The resulting encrypted String field will contain

> ```
> c(1)+c(2)+...+c(i)
> ```

> On receipt, the process is reversed to yield the plaintext String.

ARAP-Password

Attribute Number	70
Length	18
Value	STRING
Allowed in	Access-Request
Prohibited in	Access-Accept, Access-Reject, Access-Challenge, Accounting-Response, Accounting-Request
Presence in Packet	Not required
Maximum Iterations	1

This attribute is a 16-octet string designed to carry the client's response to mutual authentication of the client and the RADIUS client machine. The highest-order octets contain the dial-up user's challenge to the RADIUS client, which consists of two 32-bit numbers totaling eight octets. The lowest-order octets contain the dial-up user's response to the RADIUS client's challenge. This as well consists of two 32-bit numbers totaling eight octets.

ARAP-Features

Attribute Number	71
Length	16
Value	STRING
Allowed in	Access-Accept
Prohibited in	Accounting-Request, Access-Request, Access-Reject, Access-Challenge, Accounting-Response
Presence in Packet	Not required
Maximum Iterations	1

This attribute, found in Access-Accept packets with the Framed-Protocol attribute set to ARAP, transmits password data that the RADIUS client machine is responsible for transmitting to the user in an ARAP feature flags packet. The value is a compound string containing such information as the restrictions on a user for changing his password, the minimum acceptable password length, the password creation date in Macintosh time (32 unsigned bits representing seconds since Midnight GMT January 1, 1904), the password expiration delta from the creation date in seconds, and the current RADIUS server's time in Macintosh format.

ARAP-Zone-Access

Attribute Number	72
Length	6
Value	INTEGER
Allowed in	Access-Accept

Prohibited in	Accounting-Request, Access-Request, Access-Reject, Access-Challenge, Accounting-Response
Presence in Packet	Not required
Maximum Iterations	1

This attribute, found in Access-Accept packets with the Framed-Protocol attribute set to ARAP, indicates how the ARAP zone list for the user should be interpreted.

The value field is an integer that can be one of three values. The integer 1 signifies that the user should only be allowed access to the default zone. The integer 2 indicates that the zone filter should be used inclusively—that is, the user should be allowed to access only the zones listed in his filter. The integer 4 specifies that the zone filter should be used exclusively—meaning the user should be allowed to access all zones except those listed in his filter.

The Filter-ID attribute must also be present if this attribute's value is set to 2 or 4 in order to name the zone list filter to which the access flag should be applied.

ARAP-Security

Attribute Number	73
Length	6
Value	INTEGER
Allowed in	Access-Challenge
Prohibited in	Accounting-Request, Access-Request, Access-Reject, Access-Accept, Accounting-Response
Presence in Packet	Not required
Maximum Iterations	1

This attribute is found in an Access-Challenge packet and indicates the ARAP security module that's to be used for the transaction. The value of this attribute is an integer representing a Macintosh operating system type, which is four ASCII characters cast as a 32-bit integer.

ARAP-Security-Data

Attribute Number	74
Length	3 or more octets
Value	STRING
Allowed in	Access-Request, Access-Challenge
Prohibited in	Accounting-Request, Access-Accept, Access-Reject, Accounting-Response
Presence in Packet	Not required
Maximum Iterations	1

This attribute contains the actual challenge or response, based on the security model contained in the ARAP-Security attribute, and is found in Access-Request and Access-Challenge packets.

Password-Retry

Attribute Number	75
Length	6
Value	INTEGER
Allowed in	Access-Reject
Prohibited in	Accounting-Request, Access-Request, Access-Accept, Access-Challenge, Accounting-Response
Presence in Packet	Not required
Maximum Iterations	1

This attribute, which can be found in Access-Reject packets, indicates the number of authentication attempts a user is allowed before he is disconnected. This attribute is used primarily with the ARAP protocol.

Prompt

Attribute Number	76
Length	6
Value	INTEGER
Allowed in	Access-Challenge
Prohibited in	Accounting-Request, Access-Request, Access-Reject, Access-Accept, Accounting-Response
Presence in Packet	Not required
Maximum Iterations	1

This attribute, found only in Access-Challenge packets, tells the RADIUS client box party to the transaction whether to echo the user's response as entered by the user or whether to cease the echo. If the value of this attribute is 0, the input will not be echoed. If the value is 1, the input will be echoed.

Connect-Info

Attribute Number	77
Length	3 or more octets
Value	STRING
Allowed in	Access-Request, Accounting-Request
Prohibited in	Access-Challenge, Access-Reject, Access-Accept, Accounting-Response
Presence in Packet	Not required
Maximum Iterations	1 in an Access-Request packet; unlimited in an Accounting-Request packet

The RADIUS client gear will send this attribute inside an Access-Request or Accounting-Request packet to indicate the properties and nature of this user's connection. Among the data points collected are connection speed, transmit speed, receive speed, and any other optional information. More than one of these attributes is allowed in the Accounting-Request packet to satisfy increasing ITU pressure to allow more modem information to be transmitted that may exceed 252 octets.

Configuration-Token

Attribute Number	78
Length	3 or more octets
Value	STRING
Allowed in	Access-Accept
Prohibited in	Accounting-Request, Access-Request, Access-Reject, Access-Challenge, Accounting-Response
Presence in Packet	Not required
Maximum Iterations	1

This attribute is designed to be sent from a RADIUS proxy server to a RADIUS proxy client inside an Access-Accept packet in large, distributed networking architectures. It serves to designate which user profile to use. The value field is implementation dependent and should be read as undistinguished octets.

EAP-Message

Attribute Number	79
Length	3 or more octets
Value	STRING
Allowed in	Access-Accept, Access-Reject, Access-Challenge, Access-Request
Prohibited in	Accounting-Request, Accounting-Response
Presence in Packet	Not required
Maximum Iterations	Unlimited in Access-Request and Access-Challenge packets; 1 in Access-Accept and Access-Reject packets

This attribute serves as the method by which EAP messages are transmitted within a RADIUS packet. The RADIUS client machine places all of the messages received from the client into individual EAP-Message attributes and wraps them into a standard Access-Request packet. The RADIUS server then returns EAP messages in Access-Challenge, Access-Accept, and Access-Reject messages.

The Message-Authenticator attribute (detailed a bit later in this chapter) is required to be present if this attribute is used; this is to protect the integrity of RADIUS over EAP to the same degree that EAP affords transactional integrity on its side of the link. The Message-Authenticator must be used to protect all Access-Request, Access-Challenge, Access-Accept, and Access-Reject messages which hold one or more EAP-Message attributes.

Message-Authenticator

Attribute Number	80
Length	18
Value	STRING
Allowed in	Access-Request, Access-Challenge, Access-Accept, Access-Reject

Prohibited in	Accounting-Request, Accounting-Response
Presence in Packet	Required in Access-Request, Access-Accept, Access-Reject, or Access-Challenge packets that contain EAP-Message; otherwise, not required
Maximum Iterations	1

The Message-Authenticator attribute is used to sign packets to ensure their integrity is protected. The attribute may be used in any Access-Request, but any packet that contains EAP-Messages must also have the Message-Authenticator attribute present. The Message-Authenticator itself is an HMAC-MD5 checksum of the entire Access-Request packet, containing the Type, ID, Length, and Authenticator field, using the shared secret as the key.

As mentioned earlier in the text, some RADIUS client machines calculate the Message-Authenticator incorrectly, while others use the same attribute values for different purposes. Of course this creates a mess. It's also important to note that the use of the IPsec protocol really makes this a stopgap measure. When IPsec implementation becomes more widespread, this attribute will be made redundant.

Tunnel-Private-Group-ID

Attribute Number	81
Length	3 or more octets
Value	STRING
Allowed in	Access-Request, Access-Accept
Prohibited in	Accounting-Request, Access-Reject, Access-Challenge, Accounting-Response
Presence in Packet	Not required
Maximum Iterations	1

The Tunnel-Private-Group-ID attribute designates the group ID value for a specified tunneling session. Private groups are used to associate configured tunnels with specified groups of users. The value of the field is unrestricted and can be configured in whatever way a specific implementation requires.

Tunnel-Assignment-ID

Attribute Number	82
Length	3 or more octets
Value	STRING
Allowed in	Access-Accept
Prohibited in	Accounting-Request, Access-Request, Access-Reject, Access-Challenge, Accounting-Response
Presence in Packet	Not required
Maximum Iterations	1

This attribute is designed to specify which pre-configured tunnel a particular connection should use. More specifically, some tunnel protocols allow for multiplexing multiple connections across one specific tunnel, and with this attribute, RADIUS can inform the initiator (the client, in other words) whether the connection will be over an individual tunnel or a multiplexed tunnel.

There are specific behaviors a tunnel initiator should follow when using the Tunnel-Assignment-ID attribute:

- If a tunnel exists between the specified end points with the designated assignment ID, then the session should use that tunnel.
- If no tunnel exists between the specified end points with the designated assignment ID, then a new tunnel should be created and referred to as the label indicated in the Tunnel-Assignment-ID value.
- If the Tunnel-Assignment-ID attribute is not present, then the session should be assigned to an unnamed tunnel. If this tunnel doesn't exist, it should be created and used for all sessions that don't have the Tunnel-Assignment-ID attribute.

Tunnel-Preference

Attribute Number	83
Length	6
Value	HEX
Allowed in	Access-Accept, Access-Request
Prohibited in	Accounting-Request, Access-Reject, Access-Challenge, Accounting-Response
Presence in Packet	Not required
Maximum Iterations	1

This attribute indicates the preference assigned to each tunnel when more than one set of tunneling attributes is returned by the RADIUS server to the client initiator. The value of this attributes ranges from 0x01 through 0x1F, with the lowest value receiving the highest preference and the highest value receiving the lowest preference.

ARAP-Challenge-Response

Attribute Number	84
Length	10
Value	STRING
Allowed in	Access-Accept
Prohibited in	Accounting-Request, Access-Request, Access-Reject, Access-Challenge, Accounting-Response
Presence in Packet	Not required
Maximum Iterations	1

This attribute, found in Access-Accept packets with a Framed-Protocol attribute set to ARAP, contains the response to the dial-in client's challenge. The value is an eight-octet response to the client challenge, calculated by performing DES encryption on the highest-order eight octets of the ARAP-Password attribute's value, using the user's password as the key.

Acct-Interim-Interval

Attribute Number	85
Length	6
Value	INTEGER
Allowed in	Access-Accept
Prohibited in	Accounting-Request, Access-Request, Access-Reject, Access-Challenge, Accounting-Response
Presence in Packet	Not required
Maximum Iterations	1

The value of the Acct-Interim-Interval attribute indicates the number of seconds between each transmittal of an interim update for a specific session. The value cannot be less than 60, and best practices reveal that the value of this attribute really has no benefit to being less than 600. Serious increases in network traffic that can adversely affect performance can occur if this value is incorrectly or inefficiently set.

Acct-Tunnel-Packets-Lost

Attribute Number	86
Length	6
Value	INTEGER
Allowed in	Accounting-Request
Prohibited in	Access-Accept, Access-Request, Access-Reject, Access-Challenge, Accounting-Response
Presence in Packet	Not required
Maximum Iterations	1

The value of this attribute is the number of packets that have been lost over a given link.

NAS-Port-ID

Attribute Number	87
Length	3 or more octets
Value	STRING
Allowed in	Access-Request, Accounting-Request
Prohibited in	Access-Challenge, Access-Reject, Access-Accept, Accounting-Response
Presence in Packet	Not required
Maximum Iterations	1

The value of this attribute, read from textual characters encoded with UTF-8, indicates the physical port on the NAS machine to which to a user is connected. It is only found in Access-Request and Accounting-Request packets.

Framed-Pool

Attribute Number	88
Length	3 or more octets
Value	STRING
Allowed in	Access-Accept
Prohibited in	Accounting-Request, Access-Request, Access-Reject, Access-Challenge, Accounting-Response
Presence in Packet	Not required
Maximum Iterations	1

This attribute, found only in Access-Accept packets, indicates the name of the address pool that should be used to give an address to the authenticating user.

Tunnel-Client-Auth-ID

Attribute Number	90
Length	3 or more octets
Value	STRING
Allowed in	Access-Request, Access-Accept, Accounting-Request
Prohibited in	Access-Reject, Access-Challenge, Accounting-Response
Presence in Packet	Not required
Maximum Iterations	1

The Tunnel-Client-Auth-ID attribute designates the name of the initiator that was used during the creation of a tunnel in the authentication phase. It should be included in Access-Accept where the default authentication name is not sufficient or otherwise undesired.

Tunnel-Server-Auth-ID

Attribute Number	91
Length	3 or more octets
Value	STRING
Allowed in	Access-Request, Access-Accept, Accounting-Request
Prohibited in	Access-Reject, Access-Challenge, Accounting-Response
Presence in Packet	Not required
Maximum Iterations	1

The Tunnel-Server-Auth-ID attribute designates the name of the receiver (the server) that was used during the creation of a tunnel in the authentication phase. It should be included in Access-Accept where the default authentication name is not sufficient or otherwise undesired.

## CHAPTER 10

Deployment Techniques

It's the do-or-die moment: it's time to deploy your AAA infrastructure. That infrastructure most likely takes the form of one or more RADIUS servers (otherwise you would probably not be reading this book). This chapter is designed to cover many of the inevitable questions that come up with regard to designing a plan to deploy RADIUS servers.

First, I'll look at configuring the typical services that are offered by ISPs and corporations to their clients and then broaden that to cover extended services that support other business models. Next, I'll discuss how to maintain the service by designing a secure, highly available network. Following that are two case studies of RADIUS implementation design. Finally, I'll provide information about other RADIUS servers, available documentation, and other resources you can use to support your RADIUS operation.

Typical Services

As you've learned from the chapters on FreeRADIUS, the users that connect through your RADIUS server must be either configured into the *users* file for the RADIUS server itself or known by a remote system with which the initial RADIUS server can communicate. Anything else falls into the default connection configuration, which is sometimes known as the "catchall." Most implementations have a generic configuration that is meant for most users and a few user-specific configurations sprinkled about. In the following sections, I will provide examples of both scenarios whenever appropriate.

System Shell Accounts

The shell account, a popular service 5 to 10 years ago but less so now, is a unique type of connection that allowed access to the command line of a remote server. Users would dial in to some NAS gear, which would open a channel to the remote "shell server," and it would then prompt the user for authentication information. Assuming he provided proper credentials, the user was authenticated, got a shell prompt on the remote machine, and the NAS acted as the pass through from the client to the server. That's an important distinction, since with shell accounts the user is not provided with a direct IP address for the remote network. Since he doesn't have his own IP, he must talk with a system that does in this scenario.

There are two common types of protocols used to connect to shell accounts on machines: *Rlogin* and *Telnet*. *Rlogin* was more popular, since it was the most configurable of the two, but *Telnet* is more secure. The RADIUS server, however, must be prepared to support both protocols. An example configuration stanza from the RADIUS users file for shell account access is listed in Example 10-1.

Example 10-1. RADIUS configuration for shell accounts

```
Jonathan
    Service-Type = Login,
    Login-Service = Telnet,
    Login-IP-Host = 172.16.1.37

Anna
    Service-Type = Login,
    Login-Service = Rlogin,
    Login-IP-Host = 172.16.1.38
```

Of course, you can default the configuration—meaning all users will use the same configuration, with *Rlogin*—by using the excerpt shown in Example 10-2.

Example 10-2. Default shell account configuration

```
DEFAULT
    Service-Type = Login
    Login-Service = Rlogin,
    Login-IP-Host = 172.16.1.38
```

Direct Connect Accounts

Today, you'll find most ISPs provide direct connect accounts using a framed remote access protocol such as SLIP or PPP. With these accounts, the connecting user is assigned an IP address (or, in the case of static IP addresses, allowed to use an address) on the remote network, so that she may function like an actual node on that network.

SLIP and PPP are both available for these kinds of connections, although usually PPP is used now, since it has many benefits: it is better supported, more robust, and has quite a few link negotiation features that SLIP just doesn't have. Example *users* file configurations are shown in Example 10-3.

Example 10-3. RADIUS configuration for direct connect accounts

```
Jonathan    Password = UNIX-PW
    Service-Type = Framed,
    Framed-Protocol = SLIP,
    Framed-IP-Address = 255.255.255.254,
    Framed-IP-Netmask = 255.255.255.0,
    Framed-Routing = None,
    Framed-MTU = 1500,
    Framed-Compression = Van-Jacobson-TCP-Header

Anna    Password = UNIX-PW
    Service-Type = Framed,
    Framed-Protocol = PPP,
    Framed-IP-Address = 255.255.255.254,
    Framed-IP-Netmask = 255.255.255.0,
    Framed-Routing = None,
    Framed-MTU = 1500,
    Framed-Compression = Van-Jacobson-TCP-Header

DEFAULT    Password = UNIX-PW
    Service-Type = Framed,
    Framed-Protocol = PPP,
    Framed-IP-Address = 255.255.255.254,
    Framed-IP-Netmask = 255.255.255.0,
    Framed-Routing = None,
    Framed-MTU = 1500,
    Framed-Compression = Van-Jacobson-TCP-Header
```

Note that both users are assigned dynamic IP addresses, presumably from a DHCP-compatible device. In fact, the PPP configuration stanza for user Anna and the default configuration specifically request the NAS to assign an IP address (this was covered in the Framed-IP-Address attribute section in Chapter 3). But you, as an ISP, may provide a service for static IP usage. Or you, as a corporate IT administrator, may have deployed remote corporate applications that require a client to have a static IP address. In this case, the static IP address desired is simply specified in the Framed-IP-Address attribute in the appropriate section in the *users* file, as shown in Example 10-4.

Example 10-4. Assigning a static IP address to user Jonathan

```
Jonathan    Password = UNIX-PW
    Service-Type = Framed,
    Framed-Protocol = PPP,
    Framed-IP-Address = 66.26.224.45,
    Framed-IP-Netmask = 255.255.255.248,
    Framed-Routing = None,
    Framed-MTU = 1500,
    Framed-Compression = Van-Jacobson-TCP-Header
```

Alternatively, you may have a user who requires access from her corporate laptop with a static IP, but she may also want to dial in from a home computer to access the

Internet. In this case, you can set up the appropriate configurations very easily. You simply add the Access-Request's protocol as an item to check in the different stanzas in the *users* file for the designated user, as shown in Example 10-5.

Example 10-5. Maintaining multiple connection configurations

```
Anna         Password = UNIX-PW, Framed-Protocol = SLIP
    Service-Type = Framed,
    Framed-IP-Netmask = 255.255.255.0,
    Framed-Routing = None,
    Framed-MTU = 1500,
    Framed-Compression = Van-Jacobson-TCP-Header

Anna         Password = UNIX-PW, Framed-Protocol = PPP
    Service-Type = Framed,
    Framed-IP-Address = 66.26.224.45,
    Framed-IP-Netmask = 255.255.255.248,
    Framed-Routing = None,
    Framed-MTU = 1500,
    Framed-Compression = Van-Jacobson-TCP-Header
```

RADIUS and Availability

High availability has become the latest buzzword in Internet service. Advertisements abound for network operation centers (NOCs) with triple-capacity electric generators, dual HVAC systems, geographical dispersion, waterless combustion control, and other facilities to handle problems. While these certainly are methods to obtain and retain high availability, it seems that sometimes people lose sight of the point of such exercises: to maintain the existence and offering of services when others systems on all "sides" of the service are failing. I say "sides" to refer to the hierarchical tree in which most systems reside: there are often machines relying on a specific box, and that box relies on other boxes, and it also may work in tandem with others.

There are several strategies for planning for failure, which is the main tenet in high availability. The one most disaster-planning experts use is to account for what would be a worst-case scenario for your implementation. There are several questions to ask yourself when designing a highly available system:

Am I familiar with the normal traffic and availability of my systems?
> Am I aware of the inherent weaknesses my implementation has? You need to know what the normal behavior of your system is when deciding how best to concentrate your efforts to make it available.

Do I have a single point of failure in my network?
> That is, is there one device that provides such critical service that if it went down, users could not obtain the service they need? Single points of failure are disastrous to all kinds of redundancy because they make it moot: if your system goes down, it's completely unavailable.

What events could coincide that would overwhelm the capacity of my network?
> This scenario often comes into play when a downed system that is *not* part of the implementation causes certain events to happen inside the system. You'll see more of this later in the chapter.

How can I eliminate single points of failure?
> Would several systems performing the same task as the same time (a cluster) cure this ailment? Conversely, what systems can fail without bringing down the entire network? Prioritizing the systems to which you apply availability strategies helps you keep the cost in check while ensuring the greatest possible uptime for your system.

How can I be proactive about reducing errors and outages?
> It should be no surprise to an administrator that most errors considered catastrophic to a network are the cause of events that have been long in the making. Monitoring your systems for potential errors and their indications help to ensure problems are handled and eliminated before they even become problems.

These questions give you a fairly complete estimate of your implementation's weak points, both inside and outside of your control. Let's step through each of the questions with regard to designing a RADIUS implementation.

Determining Normal System Behavior

To establish a proper and accurate baseline for your system, there are two types of requirements you need to consider: explicit requirements, which are those mandated by your users or your company's management; and derived (or implicit) requirements, which mainly stem from the explicit requirements. For example, you may be required to make all reasonable efforts to have service restored within 15 minutes of downtime. The 15-minute window is an explicit requirement. However, you may also require that your systems have hot-swap hard drives so that you can indeed switch out a dead disc within 15 minutes. Your hot-swap requirement is derived from the explicit requirements.

Let's take a look at each of these now.

Explicit requirements

Some RADIUS implementations must deal with a constant, heavy stream of users needing its services. In this case, a measurement called packets per second is used, which quite obviously is a threshold of how many packets per second can be received and processed by the server systems. A few calculations are in order to determine what this qualification should be.

1. First, determine the number of packets that will be processed in order to start and stop one transaction. In RADIUS, this involves four packets to start the transaction and two to stop it.

2. Next, consider the average load of your system. For this example, say you have a capacity of 12,000 ports. Assume that normal operating load is about 40% of capacity, which means that 4,800 ports are in use. At peak times you may have 85% of your user base connected, which means 10,200 ports in use.

3. Then factor in a contingency for a primary circuit to go bad. Let's assume a circuit goes bad at a peak usage time, which can cause a maximum 10,200 accounting-stop packets to filter through your implementation (a worst-case scenario).

Can you handle that? It may seem like a simple question, but it's one that must be answered. It's also important to consider the number of packets per transaction, as you may be faced with a "transactions per second" constraint. In this case, RADIUS call-check may be used, which can cause more packets to constitute a single transaction. Of course, each implementation is different, so careful consideration of your environment and what your requirements are is prudent.

Some administrators believe that the primary factors in designing these systems are, of course, availability and response time. Consider the effect of a slow system: if a server is under heavy load, it will take a while to respond to a request. The client system will probably send the message again after a timeout period, which adds another packet to the load. You can begin to see the cascading effect of packet load, which likely will ultimately result in a system crash.

Another requirement to consider is the average time between system failures, or the MTBF factor. You may be familiar with this statistic from its presence on nearly all hard disc drives. For smaller RADIUS setups, in which downtime is measured in under one thousand minutes per year (close to 17 hours), then MTBF may not be as important a measure as more active monitors like packet per second and MTRS (more on that later). For larger providers, however, a figure on acceptable MTBF should be determined as part of a high-availability plan. A common figure for which companies strive is 99.999% uptime. Most systems administrators install some sort of real-time monitoring system for their systems, but the key to maintaining five-nines is tackling problems before they become problems, per se. Diligence in examining log files and using accounting data to plan and analyze usage trends should both be part of a disaster-prevention plan. However, the techniques established in this chapter aren't meant to provide for five-nines uptime. Designing for that level of availability requires consultants and expensive equipment.

Finally, while examining explicit requirements to high availability, we have to admit that all systems are going to fail at some point. There is no such thing as 100% uptime over any practical, meaningful length of time. The mean time to restore service, or MTRS, figure looks at how long it takes you or your systems to recover from an outage. This could be the most critical aspect of all of your requirements. Customers can tolerate some downtime, and few businesses run operations so important that any downtime is a catastrophic nightmare. But your customers, fellow employees, vendors, and partners will all scream if an outage is prolonged. It's likely your company earns more brownie points responding to problems quickly than it does ensuring no downtime occurs.

There are a few ways to minimize the time it takes to restore service. With hardware, it is always good practice to keep hot spares of critical components around: hubs, switches, routers, hard drives, processors, memory, and disk controllers are all parts with limited (albeit long) lives. It's also advisable to keep copies of critical system software, including the operating system and your RADIUS implementation software, close to machines on which they're installed. Regular data backups—and perhaps even more importantly, regular test restorations—should be conducted. Remember: the value of a backup is reduced to zero if it cannot be restored.

Derived requirements

The processing power of your server is one requirement that can be mandated by a threshold or directive set to maintain service availability. For example, if you need to process 25 packets per second, you require a fairly powerful server. But there may be a better solution to increase your power: since you have multiple POPs separated around a state but your RADIUS servers are in one main location, then you may investigate using several systems in parallel and building a RADIUS server cluster.

Network connectivity is also another under-compensated area. With heavy loads of traffic, it's critical to ensure your network connections are rock solid. Quality server-based network interface cards (NICs) from tier-1 manufacturers like 3Com and Intel are a must in this situation, and in most cases another NIC bound to another IP for the same machine will allow the box to spread the traffic load over the two cards. Additionally, if one dies, the other can still handle traffic and serve as an online backup until a new card can be installed.

Points of Failure

TechWeb's TechEncyclopedia defines redundancy as "...peripherals, computer systems and network devices that take on the processing or transmission load when other units fail." More granularly, redundancy is the inclusion of independent yet identical sets of components to provide an alternate way of providing a function. The concept of redundancy can be applied to individual computers, sets of computers, networks, and even entire implementation design. Moreover, systems can be as redundant as needed; as with everything, however, there is a "happy medium."

I should discuss certain terminology in regard to redundancy before proceeding further. A technique to balance and distribute loads across servers working in tandem is called a "round robin" strategy. For example, let's say I have three RADIUS servers in one POP. The NAS is configured to send calls in order to one of the three RADIUS servers; the mentality behind this is that the traffic load will be evenly placed among the three servers by choosing the next available server in the "list" upon dial-in so that no one server is operating under a much heavier load than the others.

Secondly, "failover" is a term used to describe when an administrator has ensured service availability by enabling a service to cut over to another standby server when a primary server fails. This is most commonly found in groups of two servers in one geographic location, such as a particular POP in a city. There may be two RADIUS servers, for example: one configured to handle all of the requests normally and another to take over the duties if the first fails. Hence, the RADIUS service "fails over" to the backup server. (It's been known, however, for fail-over systems not to resume back to the normal servers when the failure condition is resolved. This can inadvertently direct large amounts of traffic to your failover servers, which might not be designed to handle such a load. It's something to be aware of.)

Redundancy is often found inside specific pieces of hardware, particularly servers. Most industrial-strength servers include the capability, if not the hardware, to maintain redundancy in critical machine subsystems: power, processors, and controllers. In most cases, the computer's BIOS will detect a failure of a critical component within milliseconds and automatically cut over to the auxiliary device, which is already installed in the machine's chassis. This is one of the benefits you receive for paying extra money for a standard server-class system instead of commissioning a regular personal computer.

Hubs and switches are also critical devices that are often overlooked. Ports on these devices can suddenly fail, leaving you without any connectivity to your machine. Unfortunately, switches and other concentrators designed for heavy use in a data-center are often very expensive, so you must weigh the benefit of keeping an identical spare switch on site. Ideally, your machine will have two network cards present that are connected to two separate switches. This eliminates two probable points of failure: the port on a switch (or the entire switch, in the event of a power loss to a rack or a unit) and the NIC inside the chassis. This is cheap insurance and not very difficult to configure.

There is an issue to consider with the dual-NIC approach, however. You must have a way to route traffic between both cards. Otherwise, when one card (or concentrator port) fails, your traffic routes will fail to switch over to the functioning interface. This phenomenon is known as "convergence failure." To cure this, run a routing daemon such as *gated* across all of your interfaces. Another problem that tends to creep up is managing IP addresses. These numbers often change, and this can create havoc for system administrators trying to announce and provide these numbers to the public. It also creates issues with proxy servers and other systems that see your servers as clients. To absolve the renumbering issue, use virtual loopback addresses. These function as aliases to your real address so that your public customers and other remote clients can use these numbers to reach your system no matter what numbering it uses.

Planning to Fail

Having multiple servers ready to take over in case of failure is one of the most effective ways of combating downtime. Unfortunately, having multiple servers increases the total cost of ownership of the entire implementation, and many times management may want to increase availability but at the same time spend as little money as possible. However, budgeting for high availability systems is much like budgeting for any type of insurance, whether business or personal—you pay money up front for the time you will need it, but when you need it, you need it badly.

A fellow author and systems designer/administrator once told of the concept of building for failure. I find that a healthy attitude to take. Companies often build technology infrastructures involving systems critical to their day-to-day operation and then later discover the need for fault tolerance and uptime increase. Renovating an existing implementation to conform to strict availability standards is extremely expensive. However, up-front planning reduces much of this cost, and allows you to take high availability to a level that otherwise may have been cost prohibitive.

There are a few different levels, or "temperatures," of high availability (HA), ranging from inexpensive and least timely to most expensive and instantaneously available. It's easiest to delineate these temperatures into three groups, but that distinction made here should not be treated as a statement that other combinations of HA systems are not available. In fact, combinations are often necessary because of unique infrastructures and system peculiarities. The point of HA is to strategize your network layout and design to plan for every malicious network event and minimize downtime as much as possible.

Cold standby servers offer the least protection from outages, but they are also the most cost-effective standby systems. Most often, the cold standby RADIUS server is actually a box performing another network duty (SMTP service, for example), but the administrator installs and configures the RADIUS server software on that machine and then shuts the service down. The problem with cold servers is that the administrator must know there is a problem with the primary servers, and he must actually perform the cutover to the standby server manually. While it's not expensive at all to keep a cold standby around, it provides very limited failover services and maximum uptime during an outage.

The next step up on the availability thermometer is a warm standby server. *Warm standby servers* are most likely identical to the primary, in-service machines both in hardware configuration and software maintenance. However, these servers are powered on and able to take over service for a primary server should it go down in a matter of seconds. Software APIs residing on both machines normally can make and receive calls to determine when the standby server should take over duties from the active server.

Hot standby servers are the most expensive and most effective way to ensure your implementation has the most uptime possible. Hot backups generally run the system software actively, which means a method of synchronization is present between the active and standby servers to make sure session information and real-time data is mirrored between the two. However, the standby server is not contacted unless all primary servers have gone offline or are otherwise unable to perform service.

Proactive System Management

An equally important part of maintaining a RADIUS implementation with the least downtime possible is keeping up with your system and examining it on a daily (or sometimes even more often) basis. There is a glut of monitoring tools on the market now, and there are as many freely available open source tools that can be had for the simple price of compilation and configuration. Most of these tools profile various metrics of your system in two key areas: service statistics and system statistics.

Service monitoring is designed to see two things: whether the service is functional, period, and then what kind of load under which the service is operating. The most effective way to test the first tenet is to have a packet generator send RADIUS packets emulating an incoming NAS connection. If a response is received from the RADIUS server, I know it's operating. Beyond that, I want to see some statistics about the environment in which the service is being provided.

Logons per second
> This statistic measures the number of successful authentications (through counting the number of Access-Accept packets) per second through your system. You can also monitor the start type of Accounting-Request packets, although you lose the ability to see the reject ratio: how many requests were granted to every reject.
>
> **Look for:** abnormally high counts for this statistic. This would indicate a general network problem that would disconnect a user. He'd then attempt to reconnect, sometimes multiple times, increasing this counter and indicating a problem that needs attention.
>
> **Also:** abnormally low counts. This could indicate a network problem.

Logoffs per second
> This metric counts the number of disconnects per second from your system by counting the stop-type Accounting-Request packets.
>
> **Look for:** abnormally high numbers. It would indicate a mass network problem, a faulty NAS port, a problem with a circuit, or a bad remote-access card.
>
> **Also:** abnormally low counts. This could indicate an accounting problem, a monitoring (SNMP) problem, or an idle timeout problem.

Rejects per second
> This number monitors the amount of rejected authentication attempts per second. Coupled with smart NAS equipment, which often includes the suspected

motive behind the disconnect, you can often apply logic to certain disconnect types and determine a problem from there.

Look for: abnormally high counts. This would indicate a problem with the local user authentication database. It also may point to a problem with a remote machine's database if the RADIUS server(s) is/are acting as a proxy.

Reject cause threshold

You may decide to create and track the suspected reasons for disconnect. Then your monitoring software can increase the count for each type of disconnect as the logoff occurred, and when a certain type of disconnect reached a certain count, you would be alarmed. This is an ideal form of proactive management, in that this threshold can be set before a minor problem turns into a major one.

Look for: high abnormal disconnects. You also may want to investigate if your monitoring software has this feature embedded or included.

Total packets per second, across all interfaces

Sniffing your network interfaces and counting the packets can determine this metric. It's worth the trouble, since packets per second is a great way to monitor your performance under a known and expected load. It's also useful for historical mapping and trend analysis.

Look for: higher than normal counts. This may indicate problems such as high load, abnormal disconnects, and other difficulties which would entail packet "flooding."

Also: abnormally low counts. This could indicate a network problem, an accounting problem, or a monitoring (SNMP) problem.

The same strategies for service monitoring can be applied to monitoring the health and activity of the hardware on which the service runs. It's important to determine a baseline with these metrics, as with any other metric, since the thresholds to which you want an alarm must be set at 25%–30% above your normal system activity tolerance. Here are a few key aspects of your system that need to be checked often.

Load average

The load average depicts the average load over an entire system. On Unix machines, the load average can be determined from simply running a utility from the command line. It's important to remember that the load average most affects multiple processor machines: common practice shows that the load on a dual SMP system should never exceed 1.0 for an appreciable length of time.

Look for: an average significantly above your baseline; a load in excess of 1.0 for more than one hour at a time on a dual CPU system or proportionally larger on a larger multiprocessor system. These tend to indicate bottlenecks in your system, zombie processes, and other maladies that need to be addressed.

Memory statistics

Profiling memory usage is a trick that requires forays into more gray areas than the other metrics. Memory usage is relative, in that highly loaded RADIUS servers can use more memory and be within acceptable tolerances than lightly loaded servers. The different RADIUS servers in use, coupled with the various methods of holding packets and configurations in memory, prevent anyone from determining a single threshold at which memory use becomes rampant and detrimental. It's unique to each machine.

A better way to track memory usage is to correlate your measurements over a period of time with some of the other service metrics, such as total packets per second or logons per second, and another system metric, such as the load average. Over a period of three or four weeks you can begin to determine what an average load requires of the memory in your system.

Memory-use methods should also be analyzed. Unix and Unix-based operating systems will, by design, consume almost all of the available memory for a particular system. However, the way it uses this RAM most efficiently is by making it available as buffers. If the usage of a machine is primarily for buffers, than all is well. Any decent memory-usage utility will depict the current style of usage for a machine's memory.

Look for: an appropriate threshold for your machine. This can be determined, as mentioned previously, with time and base points on other metric. Servers saddled with 1 GB of RAM can approach 80% memory usage with more ease and less trouble than boxes equipped with 128 MB of RAM. Throwing memory at a machine is a cheap way to alleviate a usage problem, but you may want to examine other aspects of your system to determine if there is a memory leak or improper memory management in a running process.

Disk Usage

While disk space is getting cheaper by the minute in this day and age, it still makes sense to examine whether the space you already have is being used wisely. Accounting servers are notorious for accumulating gluts of information, although large user databases can occupy much space on RADIUS servers only handling authentication and authorization.

Look for: abnormally high disk-usage growth, particularly after a configuration change. Consider redundant disk arrays for extra space and added reliability and security. Also, for Unix and Linux machines, examine your partition structure, and ensure your logs and other files that need room to grow are placed on partitions with ample space.

Processes

Some monitoring systems watch processes at certain intervals, as scheduled by the Unix commands *at* or *cron*. You will want to monitor the critical processes for your server, which can depend on the software being used.

Look for: critical processes that are stopped or "zombied"; a high number of automatic alarm-restarts from your monitoring program. These events can indicate a configuration problem with your software or operating system or abnormally high loads.

Case Studies in Deployment and Availability

Once you've focused on securing the availability of your hardware and software through redundancy, you should examine making the entire RADIUS service as a whole more available. It's important to remember, however, that consultants who specialize in designing a network topology to be highly available make six-figure salaries doing just that, so to present every opportunity to make a system highly available is beyond the scope of the concept here. Like all plans for failure, you as the designer must strive to reach the "sweet spot" between cost and results.

In that spirit, I'll present two example network topologies that accomplish the most redundancy and availability without breaking the bank. I will cover the availability and redundancy strategies used in each design; then, you can take the best practices outlined here and use them as a starting point for your own design. And remember, part of being a designer is knowing when to bring in the big guns: don't be afraid to call a consultant if you realize that you're in over your head. It would simply be a waste of time, money, and system resources to continue at that point.

Scenario 1: A small, regional ISP

Raleigh Internet, Inc., is a small Internet service provider operating within the Research Triangle Park region of North Carolina. The provider offers service to residents of the region and the surrounding counties. Raleigh Internet has created points of presence in three locations: at its head office in Durham, with 1,000 ports; in a co-located telco area in Chapel Hill, with 1,500 ports; and a rented set of 2,500 ports from a network conglomerate to serve the Raleigh city proper. Their average user load is 35% on each POP, for a total active port count under normal load of 1,750 ports. They wish to provide as much service availability as possible, but the budget is certainly not unlimited and 99.999% uptime is not an explicit requirement. The ISP does need to maintain support for processing at 90% load (4,500 ports) across all its POPs without problems.

The company maintains a single set of RADIUS servers in its Durham office, along with its arsenal of other service machines for mail, personal web pages, Usenet, and additional services. It doesn't want to maintain separate RADIUS servers able to perform authentication on their own at each POP because of the administrative overhead involved in change management: for example, what if a user in Raleigh changed his password and then went to work in Chapel Hill? How would the password change propagate from the Raleigh machine to the Chapel Hill server? In addition,

Raleigh Internet needs to maintain the ability to continue to authenticate users in the event one server goes down.

The solution for Raleigh Internet would look something like the topology depicted in Figure 10-1.

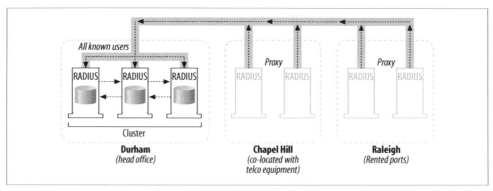

Figure 10-1. An availability solution for a small ISP

In this network design, each POP maintains two RADIUS machines that act solely as a proxy. The proxy servers are configured to send packets to the main RADIUS machines at the Durham office. The Durham office contains three RADIUS servers working in tandem with a real copy of the authentication database. Having the database on a single cluster of machines makes change management and propagation issues less of a problem. This solution also allows for the contingency of a RADIUS server in each POP going down: the remaining servers can still proxy to the cluster of real servers in Durham and continue processing AAA requests.

The ISP decided against having real servers in each POP for two reasons: one, it didn't want to invest in expensive programming and consulting expenses to rectify the propagation problems. The benefits of having five-nines uptime, at least to management, were not worth the cost of ensuring more availability, since most of Raleigh Internet's customer base is in the residential market. Their customers didn't demand such uptime requirements since having access to the Internet wasn't mission critical.

In summary, here are the key strategies involved with this scenario:

Determining a system baseline
    The nominal active load of 1,750 ports system-wide was calculated.

Managing explicit and derived requirements
    The ISP needs to be able to service 4,500 active ports at a maximum across all POPs without any special modifications. This entails having machines capable of handling such a heavy load. Hence, the three-machine cluster was specified at the Durham central office. As well, proxies at each POP ensured immediate attention to new and existing connections.

Analyzing risks of single points of failure

Since in the original design, if the RADIUS server in the Durham office went down, nothing could authenticate, the cluster was added to maintain service. As well, dual servers at each POP that work in failover mode (i.e., a primary and a backup server) ensure if one proxy goes down, requests can still funnel to the central office.

Scenario 2: A corporation with branch offices

Acme Machine Tools, LLC, is a midsize manufacturer of shop automation and general construction equipment with just over 2,000 employees. Acme has a main office in Chicago, with three branch offices in Tempe, Dallas, and Birmingham. The company has NAS gear in Tempe, Dallas, and Birmingham, each with 500 ports and a nominal active port load of about 75 ports. The company would like to support a 98% maximum load at each POP (490 ports each), for a maximum system-wide load of 1,470 active ports. The company has hired RADIUS administrators for each POP as well as one for the corporate office.

Acme wants to create a service that will allow its employees in the corporate offices to work from home and gain access to the corporate network by dialing in to each city. It also has a fleet of mobile workers that roam around the entire country while making sales calls, and they need to be granted access as well. It is assumed that each corporate employee who works from home will only dial in to the set of ports for his respective location (i.e., Jill from Tempe will only dial the Tempe number since she does not travel). However, the sales fleet needs access to the corporate network and from there, the Internet, from wherever they happen to be. It is also assumed that the work-from-home option is not offered to employees in the Chicago area.

The company wants as little administrative overhead as possible, although Acme's resources are a bit more extensive and its budget considerably larger than Raleigh Internet's plan. How is this best accomplished? Figure 10-2 illustrates the most effective solution.

Let's take a closer look at this solution. I have placed two fully functional RADIUS servers in each city's POP, with one configured as the primary, always-on server and the other configured as a backup server for failover purposes in case the primary server goes down. Based on the assumptions previously listed, I know that the users who work from home in each city are the only ones that will be dialing that POP's number. By that assumption, I can simply sort the users that need dial-in access by their city of residence and configure only those users on each city's RADIUS servers. So the RADIUS servers in each city's POP will authenticate those users it knows about.

But that leaves out the fleet of mobile workers. How will they gain access? First, I have placed a three-node parallel processing cluster of RADIUS servers—the core of the network—at the corporate head office in Chicago. These servers know about

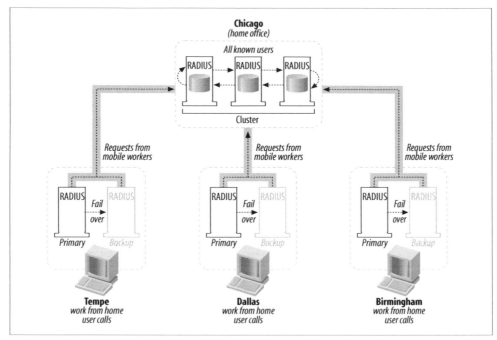

Figure 10-2. Availability solution for a midsize corporation

every user with remote-access privileges in the entire company, so these machines are effectively root servers, much in the same way that there are root DNS servers for the global Internet. The individual RADIUS servers in Birmingham, Dallas, and Tempe will be configured as clients on the root RADIUS cluster in Chicago. So when a mobile user dials a POP, and the POP does not explicitly know about those users, then the individual RADIUS server forwards the request to the root servers.

So the mobile users are happy, the work-from-home users are happy, and your administrators are happy, too—the user management in this design is a cinch since the servers in Tempe, Dallas, and Birmingham all depend on the Chicago root nodes. All the administrators have to do is keep the corporate servers updated, which automatically makes the clients rely on updated information.

In summary, here are the key strategies involved with this scenario:

Determining a system baseline
> The nominal active load of 225 ports system-wide was calculated.

Managing explicit and derived requirements
> Acme Machine Tools, LLC, needs to be able to service 1,470 active ports at a maximum across all POPs without any special modifications. Again, the POPs must be equipped with servers that can handle such loads. The accessibility of the service is more important with Acme than with Raleigh Internet, since the

workers' ability to connect to the network directly affects their ability to get corporate work done. Hence, access is mission critical.

Analyzing risks of single points of failure

I have made the network design for the remote-access service as redundant as possible. The three-machine cluster was placed in Chicago since all the POPs relied on the root servers for up-to-date user authentication information. If the corporate servers went down, employees would be denied access, so a parallel-processing cluster was deemed necessary. In each POP, the two-machine group (one primary, one backup standby for failover) was sufficient for redundancy purposes.

There are other places for redundancy to be applied (in NAS gear, for instance, or in telephonic devices), but they are beyond the scope of this discussion.

Other Things RADIUS

There are various other "mini-facets" of RADIUS that I haven't touched on in this book. This section is designed to point you to alternative RADIUS servers, special RADIUS tools that are available to help you with your deployment and day-to-day operation, and various documents that may assist you in learning more about RADIUS.

Other RADIUS Servers

There are several available RADIUS servers:

Cistron RADIUS

Written by Miquel van Smoorenburg, this server has become widely used in the free-software community. It is completely constructed from the original Livingston source. *http://www.radius.cistron.nl*

GNU-radius

This server is—you guessed it!—another Cistron server-based RADIUS implementation, although unlike the other variants a lot of the code has been rewritten. The server has a rewrite configuration file that is very convenient.

ICRADIUS

This server is a variant of the Cistron server. It includes such added features as support for the MySQL database and a front end in interactive HTML. *http://radius.innercite.com*

Navis Access

Lucent's server is an extremely flexible, expandable, and scalable RADIUS server—but it is a commercial product.

OpenRADIUS
> This server is a completely new implementation with a foundation in the "modular" mind-set, in which all program functionality is based on plug-in code that is completely under the control of the administrator. *http://www.xs4all.nl/ ~evbergen/openradius-index.html*

PerlRADIUS
> This is an effort to write a RADIUS implementation in Perl. This effort seems to be another "me-too" effort: that is, the developers are writing the code merely to say they have written the code. I see no useful benefit from this distribution and, apparently, its development has recently gone on hiatus.

Radiator
> Another RADIUS server, this is written in Perl and is designed for use in smaller implementations.

Steel Belted RADIUS
> From Funk Software, this is a commercial product that runs on Windows servers.

VOP RADIUS
> From VOP Software, this is another commercially-available Windows-based RADIUS server.

XtRADIUS
> Another Cistron server deviate, XtRADIUS supports extensions for running external programs for accounting or authentication. *http://www.xtradius.com*

YARD RADIUS
> This server is derived from the open sources of Livingston RADIUS Server Version 2.1. It has better configuration support and extended features.

RADIUS Tools

The following tools may prove useful to you as you administer your RADIUS implementation.

- The entire RADIUS attribute list is available at *http://www.freeradius.org/rfc/ attributes.html*. Each attribute is cross-referenced to the relevant RFC. This can be handy to have linked onto your management console's desktop.

- A RADIUS accounting log analysis program is available at *http://www.shenton. org/~chris/nasa-hq/dialup/radius*. This site also provides a front-end for user password changes and administration for Ascend gear.

- The FreeRADIUS people have a user addition script available at their Related Software page at *http://www.freeradius.org/related/*. They also have live links to the alternative RADIUS servers.

- Paul Gregg has created the *RadiusReport* utility, available at *http://www.pgregg. com/projects/radiusreport/index.php*. The utility, written in Perl, analyzes RADIUS logs and creates numerous reports that contain valuable data.

Attribute Reference

In this Appendix, the RADIUS standard attributes are listed in order by their attribute number, followed by the official name, the length of the attribute in the packet, and what type of value the attribute supports. Each attribute is then cross-referenced with the main body page explaining the details of the attribute.

Table A-1. The RADIUS standard attributes

Number	Name	Length	Value	Page
1	User-Name	3+ octets	String	60
2	User-Password	18-130	String	61
3	CHAP-Password	19	String	39
4	NAS-IP-Address	6	IP Ad.	52
5	NAS-Port	6	Integer	53
6	Service-Type	6	Enum	56
7	Framed-Protocol	6	Enum	45
8	Framed-IP-Address	6	IP Ad.	43
9	Framed-IP-Netmask	6	IP Ad.	44
10	Framed-Routing	6	Enum	47
11	Filter-ID	3+ octets	String	40
12	Framed-MTU	6	Integer	44
13	Framed-Compression	6	Enum	42
14	Login-IP-Host	6	IP Ad.	50
15	Login-Service	6	Enum	51
16	Login-TCP-Port	6	Integer	52
17	*(not in service)*			
18	Reply-Message	3+ octets	String	56
19	Callback-Number	3+ octets	String	37
20	Callback-ID	3+ octets	String	36

Number	Name	Length	Value	Page
21	*(not in service)*			
22	Framed-Route	3+ octets	String	46
23	Framed-IPX-Network	6	Integer	44
24	State	3+ octets	String	59
25	Class	3+ octets	String	40
26	Vendor-Specific	7+ octets	String	61
27	Session-Timeout	6	Integer	59
28	Idle-Timeout	6	Enum	48
29	Terminate-Action	6	Enum	60
30	Called-Station-ID	3+ octets	String	37
31	Calling-Station-ID	3+ octets	String	38
32	NAS-Identifier	3+ octets	String	52
33	Proxy-State	3+ octets	String	55
34	Login-LAT-Service	3+ octets	String	50
35	Login-LAT-Node	3+ octets	String	49
36	Login-LAT-Group	34	String	48
37	Framed-AppleTalk-Link	6	Integer	41
38	Framed-AppleTalk-Network	6	Integer	42
39	Framed-AppleTalk-Zone	3+ octets	String	42
40	Acct-Status-Type	6	Enum	69
41	Acct-Delay-Time	6	Integer	70
42	Acct-Input-Octets	6	Integer	70
43	Acct-Output-Octets	6	Integer	70
44	Acct-Session-ID	3+ octets	String	71
45	Acct-Authentic	6	Enum	71
46	Acct-Session-Time	6	Integer	72
47	Acct-Input-Packets	6	Integer	72
48	Acct-Output-Packets	6	Integer	73
49	Acct-Terminate-Cause	6	Enum	73
50	Acct-Multi-Session-ID	3+ octets	String	75
51	Acct-Link-Count	6	Integer	76
52	Acct-Input-Gigawords	6	Integer	146
53	Acct-Output-Gigawords	6	Integer	146
54	*(not in service)*			
55	Event-Timestamp	6	Integer	146
56	*(not in service)*			

Table A-1. The RADIUS standard attributes (continued)

Number	Name	Length	Value	Page
57	*(not in service)*			
58	*(not in service)*			
59	*(not in service)*			
60	CHAP-Access-Challenge	7+ octets	String	38
61	NAS-Port-Type	6	Enum	53
62	Port-Limit	6	Integer	55
63	Login-LAT-Port	4	Enum	49
64	Tunnel-Type	6	Enum	147
65	Tunnel-Medium-Type	6	Enum	148
66	Tunnel-Client-Endpoint	3+ octets	String	148
67	Tunnel-Server-Endpoint	3+ octets	String	149
68	Acct-Tunnel-Connection	3+ octets	String	149
69	Tunnel-Password	5+ octets	String	150
70	ARAP-Password	18	String	151
71	ARAP-Features	16	String	151
72	ARAP-Zone-Access	6	Integer	151
73	ARAP-Security	6	Integer	152
74	ARAP-Security-Data	3+ octets	String	152
75	Password-Retry	6	Integer	153
76	Prompt	6	Integer	153
77	Connect-Info	3+ octets	String	153
78	Configuration-Token	3+ octets	String	154
79	EAP-Message	3+ octets	String	154
80	Message-Authenticator	18	String	154
81	Tunnel-Private-Group-ID	3+ octets	String	155
82	Tunnel-Assignment-ID	3+ octets	String	155
83	Tunnel-Preference	6	Integer	156
84	ARAP-Challenge-Response	10	String	156
85	Acct-Interim-Interval	6	Integer	157
86	Acct-Tunnel-Packets-Lost	6	Integer	157
87	NAS-Port-ID	3+ octets	String	157
88	Framed-Pool	3+ octets	String	158
89	*(not in service)*			
90	Tunnel-Client-Auth-ID	3+ octets	String	158
91	Tunnel-Server-Auth-ID	3+ octets	String	158
92-191	*(not in service)*			

Index

We'd like to hear your suggestions for improving our indexes. Send email to *index@oreilly.com*.

About the Author

Jonathan Hassell is a system administrator, IT consultant, and computer industry author residing in Raleigh, North Carolina. He currently runs his own web hosting business, Enable Hosting, and is a columnist for *WindowsITSecurity.com* and Pinnacle's Linux AppDev newsletter. He serves as a fulfillment systems analyst for Equipment Data Associates and has worked with IBM to develop a tutorial on Apache web server optimization.

Jon is an avid movie watcher, taking in all the latest flicks as soon as he can. He also enjoys playing guitar ("at least some might call it playing," he says), writing music, and dabbling in television screenwriting.

Jon can be reached at *jon@jonathanhassell.com*. He welcomes your comments and questions.

Colophon

Our look is the result of reader comments, our own experimentation, and feedback from distribution channels. Distinctive covers complement our distinctive approach to technical topics, breathing personality and life into potentially dry subjects.

The animal on the cover of *RADIUS* is a Dolium shell. This shell is that of Orcula Dolium, one of a small family of snails. Dolium live in leaf litter or on mossy rocks on mountains such as the Alps and the Carpathians. Their shells are cylindrical, and they have rounded mouths and teeth. Their color varies from yellowish to reddish brown.

Darren Kelly was the production editor and Maureen Dempsey was the copyeditor for *RADIUS*. Octal Publishing, Inc. provided production services and wrote the index. Sheryl Avruch and Claire Cloutier provided quality control. Interior composition was done by Philip Dangler and Derek Di Matteo.

Hanna Dyer designed the cover of this book, based on a series design by Edie Freedman. The cover image is a 19th-century engraving from the Dover Pictorial Archive. Emma Colby produced the cover layout with QuarkXPress 4.1 using Adobe's ITC Garamond font.

David Futato designed the interior layout. This book was converted to FrameMaker 5.5.6 with a format conversion tool created by Erik Ray, Jason McIntosh, Neil Walls, and Mike Sierra that uses Perl and XML technologies. The text font is Linotype Birka; the heading font is Adobe Myriad Condensed; and the code font is Lucas-Font's TheSans Mono Condensed. The illustrations that appear in the book were produced by Robert Romano and Jessamyn Read using Macromedia FreeHand 9 and Adobe Photoshop 6. The tip and warning icons were drawn by Christopher Bing. This colophon was written by Linley Dolby.

Made in the USA
Lexington, KY
20 December 2010